Trusting What
You Know

Miriam B. Raider-Roth

Foreword by
Carol Gilligan

Trusting What You Know

The High Stakes of Classroom Relationships

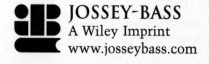
JOSSEY-BASS
A Wiley Imprint
www.josseybass.com

Published by Jossey-Bass
A Wiley Imprint
989 Market Street, San Francisco, CA 94103-1741   www.josseybass.com

Jossey-Bass books and products are available through most bookstores. To contact
Jossey-Bass directly call our Customer Care Department within the U.S. at 800-956-7739,
outside the U.S. at 317-572-3986 or fax 317-572-4002.

Jossey-Bass also publishes its books in a variety of electronic formats. Some content that
appears in print may not be available in electronic books.

Readers should be aware that Internet Websites listed in this work may have changed or
disappeared between when this work was written and when it is read.

Sections of the Introduction and Chapter Eight originally appeared in Miriam Raider-
Roth, "Taking the Time to Think: A Portrait of Reflection." *Teaching & Learning: The
Journal of Natural Inquiry and Reflective Practice*, Summer 2004, 18(3), 79-97. *Teaching &
Learning* is published by the College of Education and Human Development at the
University of North Dakota, Grand Forks (www.und.nodak.edu/dept/ehd/journal).

Sections of Chapters Two, Six, and Seven originally appeared in Miriam Raider-Roth,
"Trusting What You Know: Negotiating the Relational Complexities of Classroom Life."
Teachers College Record, April 2005, Volume 107, Issue 4 (www.tcrecord.org).

Library of Congress Cataloging-in-Publication Data
Raider-Roth, Miriam B.
  Trusting what you know : the high stakes of classroom relationships /
Miriam B. Raider-Roth ; foreword by Carol Gilligan.—1st ed.
    p. cm. — (The Jossey-Bass education series)
  Includes bibliographical references and index.
  ISBN 0-7879-7165-0 (alk. paper)
  1. Teacher-student relationships. 2. Trust in children. I. Title. II. Series.
  LB1033.R283 2005
  371.102'3—dc22   2004022758

Printed in the United States of America
FIRST EDITION
HB Printing   10 9 8 7 6 5 4 3 2 1

The Jossey-Bass Education Series

To Mark, Jonah, Emma, and Talia,
who have taught me
the deepest lessons of trust and love

Contents

Foreword

I remember my first response to seeing the evidence that led to this book. Miriam had brought her interview with twelve-year-old Jon to my class on the Listening Guide method. Asked about self-assessment, Jon spoke about the relationship between trust and truth. If you can't trust what you know, you can't know what is true—about yourself or other people. I was struck by his realization that trust, the core of relationship, and truth, which is at the center of education, are inseparable. Asked to assess their own learning, children were assessing their relationships. Emily, also twelve, speaks about lying. When the truth is something "I really won't write," she tries to avoid lying by saying nothing. Trusting what you know, saying what is true. The qualities that define personal integrity depend on the trustworthiness of relationships.

This book picks up the fundamental question about education raised by John Dewey: How do we educate for democracy? It is a question for our time. Democracy depends on people's ability to trust what they know and to say what is true. How does this capacity develop in children? How can it be fostered by teachers and schools?

Miriam begins with the voices of children. In a series of extraordinary interviews, she discovers how closely children observe classroom relationships. She highlights the shrewdness of their perceptions, the subtlety of their insights, and also the connection between what they see and hear and what they will say or suppress.

Asking questions about self-assessment, she discovers a powerful lens that brings into clear focus how the cardinal insight of a relational psychology goes to the heart of education. Voice and relationship are interdependent. Having a voice, speaking for oneself, representing oneself, saying what one knows, speaking from experience—these human capacities flourish or wither depending on the relational climate. Having relationships, living in connection with others, implies being present, being able to say in one way or another what is on one's mind and in one's heart. As developmental psychologists and neurobiologists converge in the recognition that mind and body, thoughts and emotions, self and relationships are connected rather than separate, so the shift in the human sciences from a paradigm of separateness to a paradigm of connectedness reorganizes our perception and recasts our thinking about development and education.

Taking the insights of her research into the classroom, and combining psychological wisdom with educational experience, Miriam arrives at practical suggestions and stunning observations. "When teachers lose the power to act on what they know, their knowledge loses value and their desire to know what they know about their students can wane." I have seen this dynamic play out in the course of a project on women teaching girls. When connecting with girls encourages women teachers to trust and to act on what they know, they often will make changes in their teaching that challenge educational hierarchies. As a result, moves are made to disempower the women, to keep them from acting on what they know. Some teachers resist, others retreat in the face of such pressures, the retreat taking the form of devaluing their knowledge, distancing themselves from girls, and disparaging girls in the process.

Lies, half-truths, dissociation, resistance, and retreat are political as well as psychological responses to a breakdown of trust and a failure of relationship. They are symptomatic signs of a problem that needs to be addressed. When educators take on these problems, they are acting in the service of both psychological and political health. As Miriam underscores the high stakes of classroom relationships, she offers specific guidelines to teachers: how to help children to locate their voices, how to listen carefully, how to create responsive relationships in the academic as well as the social-emotional arena, how to develop learning environments in which teachers can know their students and act on their knowledge. In challenging the separation of the academic from the relational aspects of schooling, she alerts us to the costs of current educational policies that are based on false or outdated notions of learning, competition, assessment and standardization. As the image of the separate learner and the ideal of the self-sufficient knower give way to the recognition that learning and teaching are inherently relational activities, the focus of educational attention shifts. By observing patterns of connection and disconnection, Miriam shows how teachers can work to create trustworthy classroom relationships—relationships in which ideas can "co-exist, commingle, and co-inform" one another rather than competing with and silencing each other.

On a personal level, I experienced the paradigm shift that Miriam describes—the flash of sudden insight that signals a reorganization of perception and understanding. As the mother of sons, I have attended my share of hand-wringing school conferences. Conflict between boys and school is as American as Tom Sawyer, and with my sons, I thought of such conflicts as exemplifying how "boys will be boys." Yet the incidents themselves lingered in my memory. With two of my sons, conflicts with teachers occurred in second grade. Jonathan, my oldest, refused to do his math workbook, telling his teacher that he knew how to do all the problems. When she insisted, he resisted, putting his head on his desk and falling asleep when she kept him after school. Chris, my youngest, was reprimanded by his teacher for shouting out in class on a day when a classmate was reprimanded for asking a question. "Don't be Afraid to Ask!" Chris had called out from the back of the room, reading aloud the words on a poster affixed to the wall over the black-board. "Boys will be boys," I thought at the time, taken aback by their readiness to dismiss the teacher and yet feeling a certain pride in their ability to trust what they knew and to say what was true.

Reading Miriam's work, I came to see these incidents in a different light. I realized that in both instances, my sons had read relationships accurately. They had observed a disconnection on the part of the teacher, and they had refused to participate in false relationships. It occurred to me that it is in the adamancy of this refusal that boys will be boys. Turning away from false relationships rather than acting to repair or smooth over what happened may explain why many boys become disengaged from school.

In the case of my sons, the impasse over the math workbook was resolved by the principal who summoned us to his office: my husband, myself, and Jonathan who was asked to explain his reason for not doing the work. The principal listened and in response requested Jonathan to demonstrate his ability to his teacher by doing the first and last problem on each page. I heard about the incident with Chris from his first grade teacher who had intervened on his behalf, and perhaps my sons' continuing involvement with school reflects these experiences which led them to trust that in the face of conflict a principal or a teacher would listen and respond to them.

Bringing a relational paradigm into the classroom reveals the fundamentally political and psychological nature of teaching and learning. Rather than being ancillary to the basic agenda of education, a concern with relationships is intrinsic to the goal of creating a school climate in which students and teachers are able to trust and to act on what they know and to say rather than suppress what is true. In this important and remarkable book, Miriam Raider-Roth grounds a Deweyan philosophy of educating for democracy in evidence gained from listening to children and in the insights of a relational psychology. She asks us to take seriously the challenge of developing children's ability to know what they know and to live in honest relationship with themselves and with others. Only then will they be able as adults to love and to work with integrity and to function as citizens in a democratic society.

December 2004   CAROL GILLIGAN

Acknowledgments

This book is rooted in the idea that genuine learning is predicated on trusting relationships. Such relationships made this book possible. My deepest thanks go to the students whose words form the spine of this book: Abby, Becky, Emily, Gabe, José, Maya, Sharon, as well as Jon and Daria and the other children in the pilot studies, who offered their generosity of time, wisdom, thinking, ideas, curiosities, questions, and reflections throughout the process of writing this work. They are the highest inspiration and purpose of this work. I owe a debt of gratitude to the principals and teachers at the Terrace School for their collegiality and generosity in opening up the school and their classrooms to the pilot studies and the focal research.

Carol Gilligan has been a best friend of this work and an exemplary teacher who has taught me the art, science, and magic of listening closely to human experience. Her teaching and scholarship consistently urge me to articulate the ideas that are hardest to say. My loving thanks to Harriet K. Cuffaro, who for almost two decades has taught me to experience and see the world as a teacher and who generously read the manuscript as many times as I needed her to read it. Vito Perrone's vision of education continues to provide an intellectual and ideological sanctuary for me. Eleanor Duckworth, Howard Gardner, Robert Kegan, Sara Lawrence-Lightfoot, and Annie Rogers at the Harvard Graduate School of Education; Sharon Feiman-Nemser at Brandeis University; and Patricia F.

Carini at the Prospect Archive and Center for Education and Research helped me to think carefully about the questions, methodology, theory, and writing that shaped this book. My friends and colleagues affiliated with Harvard Project Zero introduced me to the world of self-assessment, helped plant the seeds for this study, and continue to push my thinking forward.

Many thanks to my colleagues at the University at Albany, especially those in the Department of Educational Theory and Practice, for their mentorship, support, and induction into the world of academia. Many thanks to the students at the University at Albany, especially those in the "Relational Context of Teaching and Learning" seminars, who read drafts of this book, asked tough questions, and deepened my understandings of this work. Tracy Metcalf and Marta Albert provided expert research support, careful reading, and the pleasure of learning together.

The importance of teacher inquiry, group study, and collegial support proved itself repeatedly in the evolution of this book. My heartfelt thanks to the Terrace School Assessment Study Group, the New York/Vermont/Massachusetts Inquiry Group, the Robert C. Parker Faculty Study Group, the "Amazing Women" Lunch Group and the North Dakota Study Group on Evaluation.

I am grateful to the circle of friends and colleagues who supported my work in essential ways: David Allen, Eileen Anderson, Heidi Andrade, Peter Johnston, Mara Krechevsky, Carol Rodgers, Steve Seidel, and Bonnie Tai generously read and critiqued chapters and drafts of the manuscript during various stages of its development; Karen Klibanow taught me significant lessons of balance; Susan Merrett and Virginia Kahn each share a vision of schooling and activism that inspires me. My loving thanks go to Orit Netter, Connie Henry, Nancy Lubin-Levy, and Anna Rosen, for the joy, inspiration, and safety their steadfast friendships give me. I am indebted to Maureen O'Connor, Yu Zhu Teng, Rebecca Kaplan, and Erica Johnson for the love and care they have provided for my children over the years.

Generous financial support for this research was provided by the Herold Hunt Fellowship, Harvard Graduate School of Education; the James N. Snitzner Fellowship and James S. Gallo Memorial Scholarship, Harvard University; the Annie H. Ryder Memorial Scholarship, Boston Branch, American Association of University Women; and the Howard M. Soule Graduate Fellowship, Phi Delta Kappa.

Many thanks to those at Jossey-Bass for their collaborative approach to the editorial and publication process. Lesley Iura's wisdom and clear vision of this project brought this book to life. Michele Quiroga elegantly choreographed the production process. The anonymous reviewers helped me think carefully about the manuscript.

I am deeply grateful to my parents, Walter and Chaya Roth, for their consistent love, idealism, passion for writing, and the transmission of stories; they truly inspire my work. My siblings, Ari and Judy, lovingly taught me about the centrality of relationships, learning, trust, and writing in my life. The siblings who joined my life in my teenage and adult years—Katie, Steve, Lani, Daniel, and Shari—taught me how new relationships can bring new love. These are lessons that I have also joyfully learned from my nieces and nephews, Isabel, Sophie, Miko, Tema, and Elias. I thank my in-laws, Elizabeth and David Raider and "Zaydie" Alfred Raider, for their openness, love, and warm encouragement.

My children, Jonah, Emma, and Talia, have taught me the miraculousness of life and growth, the never-ending capacity of love, and the essentials of trust. They bring balance and unparalleled joy to my life. My husband, partner, and beloved, Mark, has taught me the heart and soul of trust and the myriad qualities of love. His unwavering belief in my capacities enabled this work to come to life. I gratefully dedicate this work to Mark, Jonah, Emma, and Talia for our journey as a family. *Shehecheyanu.*

M.R.R.

The Author

Miriam Raider-Roth is assistant professor of education at the University at Albany, State University of New York. She received her doctorate from the Harvard Graduate School of Education. Her research focuses on the relational context of teaching and learning and the ways that classroom relationships shape the learning process. In addition, she writes and teaches about relational qualitative methodologies as well as authentic assessment processes. Her current research, "Teaching Boys: A Relational Puzzle," investigates the ways that the sociocultural forces of gender shape teachers' understandings of relationships with their students.

A teacher for two decades, Raider-Roth has taught students of all ages, from first grade to graduate school, in the United States and abroad. Formerly a researcher at Harvard Project Zero, Raider-Roth has also worked with teachers in elementary schools in the Northeast, providing professional development workshops and facilitating faculty study groups.

She is co-editor, with Mark A. Raider, of *The Plough Woman: Records of the Pioneer Women of Palestine—A Critical Edition* (2002).

Trusting What
You Know

Prologue:
Peeling an Onion

The experience of writing this book, a study of trust, relationship, and learning has been akin to peeling an onion. As each layer of skin is uncovered, new shades of color are exposed, new textures surface. I move from the crinkly peels, to the slippery skin, to the crunchy layers underneath. Each new layer of flesh resembles the one that precedes it, but also possesses qualities—blemishes, coloring, shape—all its own. As I peel the onion, the tears start to flow. Though I may fight it, trying all the folkloric tricks to keep the tears at bay—running cold water, holding two matches between my teeth—the tears still come. I know that the tears are good. I have a fresh and flavorful onion in my hands. Still, my eyes hurt, and I secretly wish there were a way to peel onions without crying.

Studying relationship and learning creates the same type of experience as peeling an onion. In trying to understand children's conceptions of their school relationships, I create a research relationship with children who have been my students. We connect, or reconnect, in order to talk about connection—and disconnection. And so the layers of the onion begin to unfold.

In studying relationship, I experienced the onion as a phenomenon akin to the "parallel process" that can occur in psychotherapy. Simply, parallel processes occur when a patient reenacts significant aspects of her life experiences in the context of the therapeutic relationship. These reenactments can be painful, but they are often useful, because they give the therapist and the patient a shared

1

experience that can be jointly observed, discussed, and understood.[1] In this study, the parallel processes abound—in the interview process, in the analysis of the interviews, in the writing. A child describes to me how teachers look for specific kinds of answers and how they keep probing until they find them. I, in turn, find myself as an interviewer engaged in the same pursuit—asking questions until I elicit the kind of answer I can understand. Another child reflects on the words she wrote in class and finds new meanings that she did not see at first. I reflect on this same interview and realize that I see treasures that I had missed when engaged in the intensity of the interview. A child describes to me her difficulty in locating words to express her thoughts. When writing about her, I feel tongue-tied, searching to put words to my ideas.

These parallel processes—which offered me a close-up view of the students' understandings of classroom relationships as well as a chance to experience these understandings alongside the students—alerted me to the high stakes of classroom relationships. The students in this volume speak earnestly about the relationships in school that have helped them construct knowledge about themselves, one another, and the world around them. They also describe relationships and experiences in which their knowledge was undermined or pushed to a hidden space, safe from the judgment of those around them. Their stories tell us to pay close attention to the relationships in school. They are not just a "nice perk." They are the foundation of learning.

Note

1. Ekstein & Wallerstein, 1958. Many thanks to Judy Roth for offering me this source.

Part I

Considering Trust and Relationship

Introduction: Constructing a Relational Landscape of Learning

I becomes through my relation to the Thou;
as I become I, *I say* Thou.
All real living is meeting.

Martin Buber, I and Thou[1]

How do the relationships of school life shape students' capacity to trust what they know? How do children build knowledge that they can use, rely on, and articulate? What forces cause children to suppress what they know in school? Most important, what can children tell us about the ways that the relational dynamics of classroom life shape the knowledge they share in school? These questions address a discussion that is taking center stage in popular and scholarly publications, focusing on the issue of how relationships in school can fuel both student achievement and school reform. This book enters the discussion by asking *how* trust between and among teachers, students, and parents in school intersect with the kind of internal trust that students must construct in order to learn effectively.

In the chapters that follow, we will meet a small group of sixth-grade students who reveal the complexity and power inherent in the relationships of school. While they will talk about many school relationships, they focus mainly on their relationships with their teachers. In these conversations, they reveal their keen capacity to see and name both their internal or psychological processes and the interpersonal complexities they experience in school. As is evident in their ideas and stories, the children are remarkably perceptive in reading the dynamics of relationship in their classrooms and adjusting their responses to their work accordingly. They tell us that their schoolwork is as much a product of what knowledge feels safe to share as it is a product of what they know. Specifically, they suggest that they are reading their schoolwork and their classroom relationships for their safety and are giving the answers that they think their teachers, parents, and peers are able or want to hear. They tell us that their examination of the relational terrain of the classroom influences their performance in school. The students also demonstrate a remarkable capacity to articulate their understandings of how classroom relationships can shape their knowledge.

These findings are derived from a number of significant themes woven throughout the stories. The students tell us that in searching to trust what they know and those around them, they experience a tremendous relational and cognitive load that at times can feel onerous. In constructing this trust in self and others, they act politically by sharing and suppressing knowledge based on their understandings of classroom relationships. They astutely identify ruptures in relationships that undermine the very trust they are trying to build. They detect such breaks in relationship by monitoring behaviors such as teachers' responsiveness. They describe the forces that can lead to disconnecting or dissociating from their knowledge when they feel their trust in themselves or in others to be at risk. The students also recount how they construct confidence in themselves, one another, and their teachers in order to support their process of knowing. They detail how everyday classroom interactions can support this confidence and trust. In short, the students draw a complex map of the intersection of trust in self and trust in others.

Returning to the Children

This book began when I returned to the Adventurers' classroom. The airy, high-ceilinged classroom, whose walls were covered with first and second graders' drawings, collages, stories, and paintings, had been my teaching home for three years. Some of the most formative experiences of my teaching life had occurred within those four walls. I went back to this classroom in the Terrace School[2] as a researcher trying to write a portrait of how the teachers and children experienced their self-assessment work. I returned to try to understand the influence of this reflective process—a process I had helped design as a teacher.

On the last day of my fieldwork for the project, I walked slowly through the building. It was Friday afternoon and the last day before spring vacation. Children were spread all over—in the halls, auditorium/gymnasium, front office, computer room—scrubbing and cleaning. I loved the freedom and purpose I witnessed. As I left the building, I bumped into Sophie and Alice, two sixth-grade girls. I enjoyed seeing them. They had been in my first class at the Terrace School, and I had a particularly close relationship with them.

"You've been here a lot these days," Sophie said with a suspicious smile. "Are you teaching here again?"

"No," I replied. "I'm doing a research project in our old classroom." I explained that I was studying the self-assessment work that we used to do together. I reminded them that it was the kind of work in which we asked them what they learned, how they learned it, and how they felt about their learning. I asked if they remembered this work.

"Yeah," Sophie replied with a touch of disdain. "We lied sometimes, you know. Besides, it was pretty dumb."

"It was kind of dumb, but maybe it was important," Alice offered.

I drove home that Friday afternoon, thinking about Sophie's and Alice's comments and wondered about their insights. I was struck by the tension they articulated of schoolwork being both a fraudulent and an important act. Now, ten years later, I understand that the tension they surfaced held the kernel that was to become this book.

Initially, my return to the Terrace School had been to pursue some unanswered questions from my teaching days. As a teacher who had asked students to assess their own learning on a regular basis, I had been struck by the phenomenon that while some students embraced this practice, others found it difficult. I returned to Terrace as a researcher in an effort to closely observe students at work on self-assessment and to understand what factors could account for these discrepant experiences. I wanted to understand whether this work, a process that explicitly asks children to articulate their understandings of their learning, helped them build knowledge they deemed trustworthy. As I completed my fieldwork with the younger students, I became more curious about the experience of children who had gone through their elementary school experience steeped in self-assessment processes. I began to interview older children who had been my students, to get a sense of their understandings of this school practice. It was my interviews with sixth graders Jon and Emily that gave me pause. Two comments stood out in my mind:

> If the kids trust what they know, they can say, . . . "Oh, I know math. . . . I can do long division. I can do decimals. I can *use* decimals." But if they don't know what they know, [they say,] "Ooh, I'm not so sure about long division." . . . They write things that really aren't true, but they just don't know it about themselves yet. [Jon, age 12]

> If the truth . . . is something I really won't write, then instead of just not telling the truth, like lying, then I just don't say it, unless it's totally necessary. [Emily, age 12]

I wondered how a discussion of self-assessment with Jon led to his reflections about the ways students come to trust what they know and the ways this trust allows students to say what is really "true" about themselves. How did a discussion of schoolwork with

Emily lead to a discussion of honesty, truth, and lying? With the help of Emily, Jon, and a number of other children, I began to understand that self-assessment work was embedded in the web of classroom relationships and as such was a deeply relational process. I began to see that student self-assessment work was an opportune window through which to view both these "silencing" and "sharing" phenomena. Indeed, self-assessment was a process that could help uncover the intricate dynamics of relationships that play out in children's learning in school.

"Self-Assessment": Examining Both Sides of the Hyphen[3]

The practice of self-assessment, which is described later in greater depth, is one in which students examine their work in school and render opinions, evaluations, and judgments of their own work through a variety of processes and protocols. The more I talked with students about this process, the more I understood that the term *self-assessment* seemed to be a misnomer, a term reflecting an inherent paradox that teachers, including myself, were perpetuating. While we were asking students to assess their work in school and calling this work an assessment of "self," students were looking at their own learning in the context of the relationships with their teachers and their peers. How they answered the question "What did I learn?" or "What are my strengths?" was as much a reflection of what they thought their teachers viewed as important knowledge or what their peers deemed acceptable as it was a reflection of what they knew. In reality, the children's self-assessment was a relational assessment. By calling it "self" assessment, we seemed to have inadvertently covered up or hidden the highly relational quality of the work. In not acknowledging the web of relationships that encompassed this work, had we suggested to students that they do the same? In probing this issue with the students, I came to the most important learning of all. In talking about their "selves," the students described the notion of self as a complex relational construct. Upon further reflection, I wondered if perhaps the term *self-assessment* was not the problem. Perhaps it was the way we conceptualized the "learning self" that needed redefinition.

In looking at the other side of the hyphen and focusing on "assessment," I came to understand that it was not an accident that discussions of trust and truth resulted from discussions of assessment. As one student, Abby, so readily pointed out when she recently read the chapters in which she is quoted, assessment is "all about comparisons" and as such is an act imbued with the central relational issues of power, authority, and morality. Who has the power to decide if a student's work is good? Who renders judgment on a student's work, thereby deciding if she is making sufficient progress or needs remediation? When a teacher shares the assessment process with her students, how is the power relationship renegotiated? Does the student's evaluation of his work matter to the teacher? How does the teacher use the student's assessment? These questions figure centrally in the students' discussions of self-assessment. As such, we can see the inherent relational meaning in the assessment process.

In examining both sides of the hyphen in "self-assessment," it is possible to see why this practice provided fertile ground for exploring students' ideas about relationships, learning, and trust. Tapping into a practice that asks students to examine their sense of self in relation to their peers and teachers as well as issues of power and authority in the classroom, we have an opportunity to listen to the complexities that are involved in this crucial intersection.

The Process of Discovery

Unearthing the complexities of relationship, trust, knowledge, and power is the focus of this book. The findings described in the preceding section emerged from an extended research process of discovery that centered on a detailed study of nine sixth-grade children at the Terrace School.

The Setting and the People

The Terrace School is an independent school in the Northeast. Committed to child-centered, progressive pedagogy, the school uses self-assessment work as an integral part of their approach to authentic assessment.[4] The students I interviewed were of European American descent, with one child who includes Latino culture as part of his heritage. The children came from diverse socioeconomic backgrounds, as well as varied family structures.

I chose these students in particular because of their long-standing use of self-assessment work and the expertise they had developed as a result. In pilot studies, I found that sixth-grade students who had used self-assessment throughout elementary school were highly knowledgeable and held firm opinions regarding this school practice. In addition, I selected students who had been my former students because the aforementioned pilot studies (with both former students as well as children I had never taught in the school) suggested that an established trusting relationship between me and the student was a necessary context in order for students to talk with me about issues of trust. In many instances, the interview questions spurred students to talk about delicate issues such as their relationships with their teachers, friends, and family, and they referred to sensitive dynamics in their classroom and school. My long-standing relationship with the students helped create a safe context in which they could more easily trust me and my intentions and share stories that were personal in nature. Because the issue of trust was the central focus of study, creating a trusting environment in which to speak was an essential aspect of the research design.[5]

The Method

Listening closely to the students was the most important methodological task I faced. This required processes in both the interview and analysis stages that could help me listen in a careful and nuanced way.

The Interviews: Self-Assessment, Trust, and Truth

The centerpiece of this study was two in-depth interviews with each student. The interview technique blended Piagetian clinical interviewing exploration methods, which focus on the meaning of ideas, words, and terminology,[6] and a relational approach to interviewing, which centers on the meaning embedded in life experiences.[7] In the first interview, the students were asked to reflect broadly on their experiences of self-assessment work in school. The second interview asked them to reflect on two specific items: their end-of-the-year self-assessment and their assessment of their final project, a study of "Metropolis" (a city near the school).

Beginning in first grade, students and teachers at the Terrace School used student self-assessment work as an integral aspect of their ongoing and formal assessments. This work occurred regularly; students were asked to reflect on their learning process and products such as projects, math problems, and creative writing.[8] Sometimes daily, weekly, or monthly, students were asked to articulate their understandings, opinions, and evaluations of their work. They answered questions such as "What is an example of your best work?" "What work was challenging for you?" and "What do you need to work on?" Often referred to in parent conferences and narrative evaluations of student progress, the self-assessment work helped bring the student voice into the assessment process of the school. The students, thus, were highly knowledgeable about and experienced with self-assessment tasks and self-reflective modes of thinking.

As I discovered early in the pilot interviews, discussions with the students about self-assessment readily led to discussions about trust in knowledge. Following this progression, after asking students about their understandings of self-assessment, I also asked them to describe times in school when they felt they trusted what they knew, as well as times when that trust felt less present. Issues of honesty and truth consistently arose in the interviews, and these moments were explored in depth.

Listening Closely

The interview narratives were analyzed using a voice-centered relational methodology called the Listening Guide, which attends closely to the ways that relationships in people's lives shape their sense of self and ways of understanding their interactions with the social world.[9] Using this methodology to understand the children's understandings of relationships, I listened to the narratives in four distinct ways, in an effort to draw out the multiple voices the children had expressed in response to my questions. The first listening centered on understanding the nature of their stories, identifying dominant themes and silences, and locating my own responses as a researcher. The second listening focused on the ways that the students expressed aspects of self in the context of our conversations. For this listening, I attended closely to their "I" statements (such as "I want . . ., I know . . . ") and the other voices (such as "you" or "we") that might hold expressions of self. Finally, in the third and fourth listenings, I attended to the predominant tensions that arose in the narratives between knowing and not knowing, trust and mistrust, and connecting and disconnecting. In this multiple listening approach, I was afforded the opportunity to hear the students' stories from a variety of perspectives, always alerting me to the fact that in each listening, different voices of self and relationship could be heard. For a fuller discussion of the methodology used in this study, see the Appendix.

The Relational Context of School: Why It Matters

Using the tools of the Listening Guide methodology, I heard the students describe an exquisite range of experiences that help to identify the relational landscape of their learning in school. With self-assessment as their medium and the interviews with me as their canvas, the students paint vibrant portraits of their relationship with their own knowledge and the interpersonal relationships that help them learn in school.

Understanding this intersection of students' capacity to trust what they know and their capacity to trust those around them is of utmost importance for teachers and researchers as we consider and create learning practices and environments in which students can build robust understandings. In offering insight into the complexity of relational learning, the students teach us that any given school practice or structure both shapes and is shaped by the nature of relationships contained within. While we may work hard to fashion coherent curriculum, it is the relationships among all who participate that determines the quality of the learning. The way people interact, connect, talk, and play affect the knowledge that children construct and their connections to this knowledge.

These students' stories invite us as teachers and researchers to confront the ways that we connect with our students and examine whether our practices and structures facilitate the kinds of knowledge we hope that our students will build. At times, readers may find the students' stories disquieting. Readers may be left wondering whether they can live up to the high expectations that students maintain in regard to connection and relationship with teachers. By disentangling the relational complexities that one group of students articulate, this text seeks to help teachers and researchers understand the impact of classroom relationships on students' capacity to build knowledge they can trust.

Structure of the Book

This book is organized as a travelogue of my journey, in order to examine fundamental questions about relationship, trust, and learning. It is an effort to give the reader a close-up view of my observations, questions, confusions, interpretations, and further questions. As such, the chapters are organized around the important landmarks of these travels. Chapter One examines the theoretical context in which this study is located. Chapters Two through Five portray interviews with four children: José, Maya, Sharon, and Gabe. I focus on these four students in order to highlight the broad range and central features of the relational terrain of trust in self and others. In Chapters Six and Seven, I invite the voices of all the children interviewed to portray two central themes: truth and audience. These thematic paths embody key tensions that students describe in thinking about relationship and trust: knowing and not knowing, trust and mistrust, and connecting and disconnecting. Chapter Eight synthesizes the children's stories and examines their implications for educational practice.

Each step of this journey seeks to amplify the students' voices in order to help us—teachers, researchers, educators, parents—understand the ways that human relationships in school fundamentally shape children's capacity to learn, know, and trust.

Notes

1. Buber, 1958, p. 11. Many thanks to Carol Rodgers for sharing this excerpt with me.

2. To ensure the privacy of all participants in the study, pseudonyms have been used to refer to the school, students, and teachers, and some identifiers have been changed.

3. I have learned the idea of examining the two sides of a hyphen from Freeman, 1998, and Fine, 1996. The hyphen highlights both the connection and distinction between the two terms that are joined together. Freeman also describes the hyphen as a union of the person and the process.

4. van Kraayenoord & Paris (1993) articulate a useful definition of authentic assessment practices: processes that "occur in real contexts with purposeful tasks that are related to pupils' classroom curricula and learning" (p. 2). For further discussion of authentic assessment, see Allen, 1998; Black & William, 1998; Black and others, 2004; Darling-Hammond, Ancess, & Falk, 1995; Mitchell, 1992; Paris & Ayres, 1994.

5. Anderson & Jack, 1991.

6. Duckworth, 1987, 2001; Piaget, 1929/1969.

7. Brown & Gilligan, 1992; Eisner, 1998; Kvale, 1996; Seidman, 1998.

8. For further reading on the purposes and practices of self-assessment in the classroom context, see Andrade, 2003; Andrade & Boulay, 2003; Black, 1995; Black & William, 1998; Black and others, 2004; Bruce, 2001; Hansen, 1992; Hebert, 1992; MacLean, 1983; Paris & Ayres, 1994; Perrone, 1991; Ross, Hogabaum-Gray, & Rolheiser, 2002; Seidel and others, 1997; Stiggins, 2002; Tierney, Carter, & Desai, 1991; van Kraayenoord & Paris, 1993, 1997; Veenema, Hetland, & Chalfen, 1997; Walker, 2003; Walters, Seidel, & Gardner, 1994; Zessoules & Gardner, 1991.

9. Brown and others, 1988; Brown, 1998; Brown & Gilligan, 1992; Gilligan, Brown, & Rogers, 1990; Gilligan, Spencer, Weinberg, & Bertsch, 2003; Jack, 1993; Rogers, Brown, & Tappan, 1993; Taylor, Gilligan, & Sullivan, 1995; Tolman, 2002; Way 1998.

1

Trusting Relationships, Trusting What You Know

Trust has become a popular word in educational discourse these days. This is a fascinating phenomenon, given the current political climate of education, which is deeply distrusting of administrators, teachers, and children. As a society, we no longer trust principals to make curricular decisions for their schools, as is evidenced by districtwide, citywide, and statewide curricular initiatives such as teacher guides, decisions to purchase uniform textbooks, and curriculum plans for all teachers. We no longer trust teachers to make curricular and classroom decisions, as is evidenced by the widespread implementation of standardized curricula. The aggressive proliferation of standardized testing similarly communicates our profound cultural distrust of teachers' capacity to teach. The message proclaimed by these tests is that teachers do not know what children need to learn nor can they figure out how to assess whether children are indeed learning. Finally and most disturbingly, we are losing trust in children's drive to learn, as is evidenced by the implementation of high-stakes testing across the country, which suggests that unless children are threatened with the dire consequences of failing or not graduating, they will not learn.

It is in this climate that we have seen a publishing flurry surrounding the notion of trust.[1] In an educational climate that has devastatingly eroded this foundation of the teaching-learning enterprise, teachers and researchers are assiduously working to grasp, describe, resurrect, recreate, or otherwise hold on to what we know sustains human capacity to construct knowledge.

This book enters this discourse on trust with a story and a theory. The story in this book, offered in the form of conversation between children and a researcher, paints an illustration, rich in design and detail, of what trusting relationships with self, peers, and teachers look like. It portrays the landscape of the relational context of teaching and learning. The telling of this story is the centerpiece of this book and will be found in the chapters that follow.

The theory goes something like this: our deepest hope for our children is that they will construct knowledge in school about themselves, their community, and the world that is robust, resilient, and creative. This knowledge will help them become members of society who can improve our world, who can participate in our democracy, and who can take responsibility in an increasingly complex society. Children must learn to trust this knowledge so that they can use it, take risks, and allow it to grow and change. They need to trust what they know, because as they grow, it is this knowledge that will help them form the relationships that will sustain them as adults—relationships with friends and partners, relationships in their work world, and relationships with community and culture at large.

The theory continues: for children to develop trustworthy knowledge, they must learn in the context of trustworthy relationships. School is often children's first community outside of home, in which they learn the give and take of communal living, of getting along, of sharing, of listening to divergent opinions, of building new ideas in a social environment. The interconnections between trust in self and trust in others are complex and strong. I will argue in this chapter that the learning process is inherently relational; it is a process embedded in students' braided relationships with self, teachers, and peers. The prevailing political voices assert that testing children will build the foundation of strong knowledge;

in contrast, this theory argues that resilient, trustworthy relationships in school are the bedrock of learning.

The Relational Learner: Toward a New Understanding of Schooling

The theory of this book posits a learning self that is inherently relational. Drawing on the work of philosophers, psychologists, and educational researchers, this theory took form while I was listening to
the stories of the students in this book. José's words illustrate the
notion of the relational learning self expressed by the students:

> You tell them what you're good at, and they tell you what
> they think you're good at, and you can make something
> out of that. It's like they have the spice and you have the
> whole ingredient, and if you put it together, . . . you have
> yourself.

José's eloquent statement illustrates that in the interchange between teacher and student, "something" meaningful is made; "you
have yourself." He tells us that in the relational interchange of the
classroom, children's selves continue to be constructed. With ele-
gant simplicity, José's comments reveal a complex idea that represents a significant shift in paradigm for both psychological theory
and educational practice: that the learning self is constructed and
develops *within* the relationships of classroom life. Comments such
as José's also triggered a fundamental shift in my own thinking as a
teacher and researcher.

The very first paper I wrote in graduate school that investigated
the effect of self-assessment work on student learning was called
"Encouraging Autonomous Learners." When I compare that title
with the title of this volume, I see tangible evidence of the paradigm
shift I experienced in doing this research. Early in my research, I
hypothesized that student self-assessment work stimulated learners

to become more autonomous in their thinking, less dependent on the opinions and judgments of teachers and peers. This was a hypothesis with strong support in the literature on student self-regulation.[2] Yet the students in this study described self-assessment work as an illustration of their evolving understandings of the ways that classroom relationships shaped their learning. My early assumptions grew out of the traditional psychological notion of the development of self—that the goal of development was individuation and separation of self. Even in the most popular sociocognitive conceptions of schooling, the goal of interaction and social relationships was the internalization or appropriation of the lessons learned. The model suggests a taking in of the outside world, of making it one's own.[3] This is the pinnacle of development. Yet the students in this study challenge this notion of development. Their stories and ideas about classroom relationships reflect an alternate understanding of the learning self; it is a relational learning self.

In traditional western psychology, the achievement of autonomy, individuation, and separation from those most beloved has been viewed as the highest degree of development of the human self.[4] Over the past three decades, contemporary relational theorists have sought to redefine the notion of self and its development.[5] In this effort, researchers and clinicians have rethought conceptions of psychotherapy,[6] psychoanalysis,[7] infant development,[8] boys'[9] and girls'[10] development. A common thread running through this relational orientation is that the growth of the human self is embedded in and inextricably linked with relationships with others, particularly parents, caregivers, and partners. In this orientation, development of self is asserted not by autonomy and separation but rather by construction, defining, and refining of relationships. Jean Baker Miller and Irene Stiver articulate this notion of self and relationship clearly:

> In our view, the goal of development is not forming a separated self or finding gratification, but something else

altogether—the ability to participate actively in relationships that foster the well-being of everyone involved.
Our fundamental notions of who we are are not formed
in the process of separation from others, but within the
mutual interplay of relationships with others. *In short,
the goal is not for the individual to grow out of relationships,
but to grow into them. As the relationships grow, so grows
the individual.* Participating in growth-fostering relationships is both the source and the goal of development.[11]
[italics added]

The children in this book validate Miller and Stiver's hypothesis by describing how the aspects of self that they assert in school
grow and wither in the relational dynamic of their classrooms. They
suggest that their reading of these relationships not only shapes
what can be said and known within those relationships but can also
support and stunt the development of self that happens within those
relationships.[12] This notion of the relational self can be seen most
profoundly in the students' examination of teachers' motives, expectations, likes and dislikes, and assumptions. In such an examination,
the students understand that teachers "experience" them and form
conceptions of students' sense of self that may or may not conform
with the students' own conceptions of self. Further, the extent to
which students can access their teachers' conceptualizations shapes
the way they respond to their teachers, the knowledge they share,
and the internal truths they juggle.

Essentially, a central aspect of self, the relational learner, is constructed within relationships. Just as the theory of the relational self
postulates that the self is born and develops in the cradle and life
of relationships, so the notion of the relational learner postulates
that the learning self is constructed and developed within the relationships of school. In both constructs, the developmental marker
of growth is participation in mutually empathic, "growth-fostering"
or learning-enhancing relationships.[13] That is, the fundamental

relationships of school shape the ways that students learn to see themselves as effective participants in the learning process who have the capacity to develop their own ideas, articulate these ideas, and participate in collective thinking.

This paradigm does not ignore students' individuality or need to assert and construct their own meaning of their experiences. Rather, this approach acknowledges that an individual's construction of meaning is embedded in the web of relationships in school. Drawing on the work of Antonio Damasio, Carol Gilligan describes the "core sense of self" as "a voice, the ability to initiate action and to register experience."[14] This core sense of self possesses the capacity for "awareness" of registering or making meaning of the experience. This awareness is akin to knowing what you know, being connected to your own thoughts, feelings, emotions, ideas, and curiosity. When a person is most wide awake,[15] most aware, present, she can trust this knowledge; she is fully connected. As the children in this study tell us, the construction of this awareness of their own experience is inherently woven into the tapestry of school relationships. As such, the relational learner is one who initiates action, makes meaning of his experience, and develops awareness of this experience in an ongoing, mutually regulatory web of school relationships. To separate the core sense of self of the learner from the flow of learning relationships would be, in Gilligan's words, "psychologically incoherent."[16] John Dewey echoes this notion of psychological incoherence in the divided self. When the self is split or divided, the self becomes "a divided world, a world whose parts and aspects do not hang together, . . . at once a sign and a cause of a divided personality. When the splitting-up reaches a certain point we call the person insane."[17] In explaining Dewey's ideas, Harriet Cuffaro suggests that "self is not an isolated being. It is always of and with others."[18] In the context and constant interplay of school relationships, the student develops her learning self. It is our mission as teachers to help students construct and maintain unified learning selves that offer them the opportunity to construct the strongest, most trust-worthy knowledge.

The Place of Relationships in Learning

To unpack this notion of the relational learning self, we must come to a shared understanding of the term *relationship*. My understanding of relationship is drawn from multiple disciplines that cross the boundaries of philosophy, psychology, and educational theory.

Relationship with Self

First, let us consider relationship in the context of a student's connection to self, his own knowledge and learning. John Dewey's theory of reflective thinking offers a useful construct for considering this facet of relationship: relationship with one's thinking is a process of making connections between previous knowledge and new ideas one confronts. Dewey suggests that learning depends on the connections that a student makes between past experiences and present challenges.[19] He teaches us, "Increase of the store of meanings makes us conscious of new problems, while only through translation of the new perplexities into what is already familiar and plain do we understand or solve these problems. This is the constant spiral movement of knowledge."[20]

Dewey's theory of reflective thinking emphasizes that the meaning humans make of experience is dependent on the connections we can make with what we have known and experienced in the past. There is an integral process of making connection with self that underlies this process. This view of knowledge construction is aligned with Damasio's notion of "core sense of self."[21] In the process of making connections between past and present experiences, a student develops a relationship with her knowledge as well as with her own self as an active agent in her learning.[22] If we consider relationship with self as a process of making connections, both cognitive and affective, then it is important to identify the forces that facilitate, impede, and shape these connections.

Relationship with Others

As I discussed earlier, the human sense of self is deeply embedded in and inherently connected with the primary relationships in a person's life.[23] In fact, separating this discussion into the categories of "relationship with self" and "relationship with other" is an artificial separation, necessitated by the need to clearly define the notion of relationship. In infancy and toddlerhood, significant relationships, such as those with primary caregivers, begin to shape children's relationship with self. When children enter school, their relationships with self continue to be shaped by their school relationships (relationships with peers and teachers).[24] In this context, students' relational learning selves are asserted and continue to grow. It is these learning relationships that can both help students connect to what they know and lead them to disconnect or dissociate from what they know.[25]

These learning relationships are the second facet of relationship to consider. Beginning again with the philosophical underpinnings of relationship, John Dewey positions school relationships as central to the aims of education in two ways. First, in educating children to become active members of a democracy, classrooms and schools become laboratories in which to learn the intricacies of human relations that form the foundation of a democratic society. As Dewey so eloquently states, "The subject matter of education consists primarily of the meanings which supply content to existing social life."[26]

Nel Noddings also sees classroom relationships—particularly the teacher-student relationship—as a fundamental experience from which to learn the ethics of living in the greater society. She characterizes the relationship between teacher and student as one based on the ethic of care.[27] In describing the teacher as the "one-caring" and the student as the "cared-for," Noddings theorizes that the teacher's aim in education is "to preserve and enhance caring in herself and in those with whom she comes in contact."[28] Therefore, the relationship between the teacher and student must personify the ethic of care, in which the teacher is engrossed in the student's learning and the student is responsive, indicating that he has received the teacher's care and has been shaped by it.

In addition to readying students to become active participants in society, interpersonal relationships in school also serve a second purpose: they are the essential foundation of learning. Dewey views the individual as a "being-always-in-a-situation" and the transactions that occurs between an individual and the social environment as the bedrock of knowledge.[29] He theorizes that an individual child's communication with her classmates and teacher is a fundamental way that knowledge is built.[30]

The notion that knowledge is embedded in social interactions is also an idea long espoused by sociocognitive theorists.[31] A fundamental thread running throughout this psychological theory is the argument that knowledge is formed or constructed in interaction with peers, mentors, and the environment and is subsequently internalized for independent use. Research in student self-regulation extends this theory into the realm of academic performance, arguing that students' academic competence develops in the social world and gradually moves to sources in the self.[32] These studies are helpful to this discussion in that they demonstrate an inherent link between interpersonal interactions and cognition and argue that knowledge is built within the surrounding social world. This research, however, does not help us understand how human relationships contribute to the construction of trust in knowledge.

That knowledge is born and shaped in the cradle of human relationships is an idea pioneered over the past two decades by relational psychologists.[33] This field of scholarship posits that psychological growth is embedded in relationships and human development can only be understood in the context of relationships. That is, in order to see how individuals make meaning of the world around them, we must understand how the forces of human relationships shape their experiences of that world. Carol Gilligan's work in this domain is especially helpful in explaining the theoretical underpinnings of how relationships can shape knowledge.[34] She grounds her theoretical orientation in three phases of human development in which these negotiations can be clearly seen: infancy, boys' early childhood, and girls' adolescence. Gilligan points to infancy research that demonstrates that the infant's world is one of relationship.[35] Not only do infants need their relationships with their caregivers in order to survive but they are also able to affect and change these relationships. They depend on these relationships to help them make sense of all of the stimuli that surround them. Edward Tronick and Katherine Weinberg argue that the capacity to trust knowledge begins in the mutual parent-infant communication cycle.[36] As parents and infants become increasingly skilled in reading each other's cues, in expressing needs and having needs met, infants learn that they are effective communicators and that their caregivers are dependable.[37] The notion of "repair" is central to this idea of mutuality. When parents misread an infant's cue—for example, misreading a hungry cry as a signal to change a diaper, the infant learns to modify his sounds and parents learn the signals that help them regain their synchrony. The notion of mutuality arising from this research suggests that in this active communication between parent and infant—the preeminent teaching-learning relationship—children learn to trust both their perceptions and their communications and develop trust in their parents' capacity to respond. This research demonstrates the inherent link between trust in self and trust in others.

Boys' early childhood is another watershed moment in development at which we can view the ways that relationship shapes emerging knowledge. Gilligan and her colleague, Judy Chu, found that preschool and kindergarten boys negotiate a delicate balance between holding on to what they know to be true (their desire for intimate relationship with peers, parents, and teachers) and complying with the demands of patriarchal forces that surround them (that to be a boy means to break free of the very relationships that sustain them). In this negotiation, boys can disconnect or dissociate from knowledge they hold in order to yield to societal forces.[38] A similar phenomenon can be seen in girls' adolescence. Research over the past two decades has found that when girls enter adolescence and encounter relationships that demand conformity with standards that differ from their own, they are faced with complex psychological decisions that often cause them to dissociate from what they know.[39] Girls may disconnect from knowledge of themselves, disconnect from understandings of social relationships, or conduct a delicate balancing act of negotiating these different kinds of knowledge, depending on the forces they confront.[40]

The studies of both boys and girls point clearly to the ways in which the forces of human relationships shape children's capacities to hold and disconnect from what they know. These findings are supported by other relational psychologists who examine the connections between trusting relationships and trusting self and knowledge.[41] Researchers such as Jean Baker Miller, Irene Stiver, Judith Jordan, and Terrence Real who study relational functioning and health, have found that interpersonal failures—when people feel unsafe in relationships or when relationships lack mutuality—are a driving force in pushing people to disconnect from their knowledge and relationships.[42] Moreover, the key to relational awareness and health is a repair of these disconnections, a coming to know of that which is deemed unacceptable.

The research in relational psychology highlights the interwoven nature of knowledge of self and knowledge of others and provides insight into the psychological processes involved in connecting and disconnecting from both knowledge and significant human relationships. While a portion of the research just discussed was conducted in schools, it did not center on the ways that school relationships shape student learning, nor did it examine the nature of school practices that can support relationships in which students

can bring the full spectrum of their knowledge and diminish the
need for disconnecting; these were not the purposes of the studies.
Yet, they persuasively suggest that relationships shape emerging
knowledge. The next step in this line of research is to bring these
theoretical ideas to the world of school. This step requires that we
address a key question: How do school relationships shape children's
capacity to trust what they learn and know?

Developmental, sociocognitive, and school psychologists also
laid the groundwork for examining the interplay between school
relationships and student learning. Focusing especially on the impact of these relationships on student motivation, achievement, and
engagement in school, researchers have found that positive school
relationships significantly affect the quality of student learning.[43]
This research, mainly large-scale studies, demonstrates a trend at
all levels of the educational cycle—from preschool through high
school—that the interpersonal relationships of school shape students' achievement in subject matter performance such as mathematics[44] as well as students' preparedness for the tasks required of
schooling.[45] In addition, these studies reveal an inherent connection between students' experiences of schooling and their social-
emotional functioning, which is largely dependent on the quality
of their school relationships.[46] These studies offer a broad sweep of
the terrain of relationships in school and invite closer investigation of *how* school relationships shape the learning process.[47]
Investigating the etiology and evolution of trust in school relationships offers us one perspective on the intersection between
relationships and learning.

Trust in Self and Knowledge

I begin by considering the notion of trust in self and one's own
knowledge and root my understanding in the definition rendered
by the children of this study. The students explain that trusting
their knowledge means that they can discuss, use, and depend on

their understandings in order to build new ideas as well as identify concepts that they do not understand. When they do not trust their knowledge, they feel worried that they are unable to depend on their ideas, build new understandings, or articulate what they do or do not know. When they do not trust, students worry that they have lied or concealed the truth about themselves to their teachers and peers.[48]

The definition of knowledge employed in this study emerges from the students' varied references to knowledge throughout our discussions. This definition encompasses the three pivotal aspects of the teaching-learning relationship as defined by David Hawkins in his seminal essay "I, Thou, and It":[49] the teacher, the student, and the subject matter. When the students in this study discussed knowledge, they referred to what they knew about themselves: their thinking, feelings, interests, passions, curiosities, doubts, and confidences. They also described what they knew of others: their relationships and their reading of others' intentions, motivations, expressions, and communications. Finally, they described their knowledge of the subject matter of school: the cognitive, academic, intellectual, physical, artistic, and musical ideas they had encountered. Echoing Dewey's idea of the "constant spiral movement of knowledge,"[50] they described knowing as a dynamic process that was in constant interaction with self, others, and the environment.

Trust in Relationships

Just as relationship with self is inherently linked to relationship with others, so too is trust in self rooted in trust in others. I build my understanding of trust in others on the work of philosophers, psychologists, and educators as well as insights from the children who have educated me in my work as a teacher and researcher. When considering the place that trust holds within human relationships in school, it is useful to delineate the features of a trustworthy teaching-learning relationship. There are four central features: (1) the teacher's capacity to be connected to the student, (2) the teacher's genuine interest in nurturing students' own ideas, (3) collaborative study on the part of teacher and student, and (4) an environment in which trust can prevail.

Teachers' Connectedness

The first feature of trust rests on the teacher's capacity to be connected to the experience of the student.[51] This connectedness rests squarely on a teacher's willingness and ability to be sensitive to and empathic toward a student's social, affective, and cognitive experience in school. The notion of connectedness has been closely examined by relational psychologists[52] and described as having four central aspects: mutual empathy, relational authenticity, inter-subjectivity, and mutuality. Janet Surrey describes mutual empathy as the experience of "seeing the other" and "feeling seen."[53] She describes a reciprocity in this process in which both people must be visible to the other and sense that they are seen. Jean Baker Miller and her colleagues describe relational authenticity as "moment-to-moment responsiveness"[54] in which there is an effort by each person in the relationship to represent themselves "with fullness and truth."[55] In their classic study, Belenky, Clinchy, Goldberger, and Tarule describe connectedness in teaching as the capacity to "enter into each student's perspective."[56] Jordan speaks of this capacity as "inter-subjectivity," or the capacity to attend and respond to the "subjective inner experience of the other at both a cognitive and affective level."[57] Finally, mutuality, as discussed in the previous section, has been theorized most coherently by the infancy scholars and is central to the concept of connectedness in teaching in that it represents the communication cycle by which teachers and students learn the power of communication and response. As Noddings suggests, this kind of feedback loop, through which teachers and students can read the way their expressions of care have been received by the other, is central in the teaching-learning relationship.[58]

When thinking about connectedness in the teacher-student relationship, we can ask these kinds of questions: When a student is in distress in a classroom, how well can a teacher listen for the roots of the distress? When a student acts out or resists the teacher's agenda, how well can the teacher observe the underpinnings of the unrest? How well can a teacher elicit and recognize a student's intellectual passions and create opportunities for the child to act on them? How genuine and authentic are teachers in their relationships with their students? An eight-year-old boy recently described a young teacher in his school as the "best teacher in the school." Curious about his standards for teaching excellence, I asked him what made her the best teacher in the school. He replied clearly: "When she says hello to me in the hall, she says it like she really means it." His comment illustrates how closely children monitor a teacher's connectedness to their well-being.

Connectedness is a central aspect of a trusting teaching-learning relationship because it is from this standpoint that student and teacher learn to know each other at fundamental levels. The teacher attempts to assume the subjective experience of the student. The student, in turn, feels that she has been seen or recognized and that a place has been made in the classroom for her, in all her complexity. Students learn that they can be effective communicators, that their needs can be met, and that they too can meet the needs of others. They learn that learning is a relational enterprise.

Teachers' Genuine Interest

The second quality of a trustworthy relationship is a teacher's genuine interest in nurturing students' own ideas. This notion is anchored in the work of Eleanor Duckworth and David Hawkins. Duckworth describes this quality as allowing students' own "wonderful ideas" to emerge in the classroom.[59] She argues that it is the opportunity for children to have wonderful ideas of their own that is the essence of intellectual development. In nurturing children's ideas and helping them extend their emerging theories, Duckworth suggests that teachers give children "reason"—they attempt to understand the meaning in children's words or behaviors—in order to take their thinking "one step further."[60] David Hawkins links teachers' interest in children's thinking with the creation of trust.[61] He argues that when teachers value students' ideas, teachers create a "compact of trust." The nature of this compact is one in which "the teacher seeks to extend the powers of the learner and promises to abridge them only transiently and to the end of extending them."[62] In doing so, teachers acquire authority. Hawkins's idea of authority is contrary to a traditional conception in which a teacher may look for obedience and compliance as indications of his authority.

Not too long ago, I observed this notion of authority in a preschool classroom. A child had grabbed hold of some multicolored masking tape and begun, carefully and attentively, to make colorful tape designs along the legs of a chair, looping the tape around the leg to create a barbershop-pole pattern. Many teachers might have chastised the student for tampering with classroom furniture. This gifted teacher stood back and watched the child's purposeful construction, offering him the opportunity to explore the qualities and aesthetics of this material. Allowing the construction to grow, she provided more tape and other materials and watched as other children joined the project. By the end of the week, the children had produced what they called a "sculpture," which they displayed with pride on classroom project night.

The quality of the trust between this teacher and her students is rich indeed. The teacher trusted the students' intentions to be constructive and creative, and the students trusted the teacher to be interested in, supportive of, and provider of the requisite materials for their explorations. This story suggests that in order for students to trust that their teachers are genuinely interested in their learning, teachers must express curiosity about the ideas that students generate and allow opportunity for exploration of these ideas.

Teacher-Student Collaborative Inquiry

The third quality of trust is that of collaborative study between teacher and student. This idea is eloquently argued by R. P. McDermott in describing the social contexts that support student learning.[63] McDermott suggests that trust emerges when teachers and students engage in a shared focus of study that involves collective work and active exchange of ideas among all members of the classroom community. Again, this idea shifts the locus of authority from the teacher as "all-knowing" to the teacher as a learner who is asking questions and seeking, together with her students, to craft new knowledge.

In thinking about shared inquiry as a fundamental feature of trust, Hawkins's notion of the "It," or subject matter, as a pivotal point in the triarchic nature of the student-teacher relationship is especially clear. That is, for a trusting relationship to emerge, a study of central importance to both the student and the teacher is essential. A graduate student of mine recently recounted how the introduction of a classroom pet, a frog, shaped the environment of her multi-age classroom. She discovered that through the introduction of this animal into her classroom, a new focus of study emerged for her and the students. They became partners in the discovery of everything from the climate necessary for the frog's survival to the biology and anatomy of the animal, from its feeding habits to its preferences. As she watched study of the frog deepen, she began to notice new social relationships emerging, and she noticed the quality of the trust between her and her students growing more profound. As the collaborative study of the class pet became more intense, the relationships in the classroom grew, as well.

An Environment of Safety

The fourth aspect of trustworthy relationships involves creating an environment in which trust can prevail. The key feature here is the quality of safety. Students in this study explained that they were only prepared to share reflections on their learning if they knew that teachers would hold these conversations in confidence and not reveal them in front of others. Towler and Broadfoot likewise identified privacy, confidentiality, and invitations to challenge teachers' authority as key features of safety.[64] Sustaining an environment in which students and teachers feel safe to build new knowledge requires avenues for protected conversation and exchange of ideas.

To create safety for all voices, including dissenting ones, to be heard, there must be permission to disagree. This is an understanding recently articulated by a group of teachers at the Robert C. Parker School in upstate New York, who joined with colleagues in the area to study the ways that issues of race played themselves out in their school. In our studies, we came to understand that while "safety" can be protective for some students, it can be a silencing force for others, making it difficult for students to express dissenting opinions. We saw that the ideal kind of safety was one that allowed people to "be dangerous," to take risks, to voice that which had not been said. We also saw that the definition of safety changes for each individual, reflecting that person's sociocultural identity, the power dynamics in the classroom, and the surrounding community.[65]

Underlying these four qualities of trustworthy relationship is the value of freedom. An environment in which trustworthy relationships can thrive requires that students be free to make choices that reflect their interests, to disagree with teachers' perspectives, and to take risks with ideas that are new and not fully formed. In short, trustworthy relationships in the classroom can be understood as a commitment to honoring both privacy and dissent, sharing authority among the members of the class, and creating a collaborative focus of study through which teachers and students can actively form a community of learners.

Trust and Relationship, Trust and Knowledge

There is a "chicken-and-egg" quality to a discussion of trust and relationship. While discussing relationship, we see that trust is an inherent component of this human connection. While discussing trust, we see that it is lived out in the context of interpersonal relationships. Rather than viewing one concept as the cause of the other, we can see trust and relationship as inextricably linked, as mutually dependent. At times, the distinction between trust and relationship can feel artificial or imposed. Yet it is a distinction worth considering in an effort to understand the human context that best supports children's learning. Similarly, the distinction between knowing something and trusting that knowledge is a subtle and important one to consider. In the following chapters, the students describe these distinctions, highlighting that trust is a quality that makes both relationships and knowledge robust and enduring. This discussion seeks to disentangle the complexities involved in building this trust.

Essentially, children come to school with many processes of knowing fully in gear. They learn quickly that some of what they know cannot be spoken in school, while other kinds of knowledge are invited and have hallowed spaces in the classroom. That is, the relationships in school are critical contexts for shaping students' connections to what they know. These relationships shape the ways that students can trust what they know. In the chapters that follow, the students and I talk openly about the ways that the relational contexts shape their learning, craft what they know, and facilitate a confidence, dependability, durability, and trust in what they know.

Notes

1. See Bryk & Schneider, 2002; Cook-Sather, 2002; Howes & Ritchie, 2002; Koplow, 2002; Meier, 2002; Perrotti & Westheimer, 2001; Watson & Ecken, 2003.

2. Paris & Newman, 1990; Patrick, 1997; Schunk & Zimmerman, 1997; Schunk, 1990, 1996.

3. Piaget, 1952/1963, 1970; Rogoff, 1990; Schunk & Zimmerman, 1997; Vygotsky, 1978; Wertsch, 1985.

4. Erikson, 1963; Kohlberg, 1984; Maslow, 1970.

5. For a thorough discussion of relational psychological theories, see Spencer, 2000.

6. Gilligan, Rogers, & Tolman, 1991; Jordan and others, 1991; Miller and others, 1999. Thanks to Judy Roth for sharing the Miller source with me.

7. See Spencer, 2000, for a clear overview of the relational psycho-analytic theory.

8. Murray & Trevarthen, 1985; Stern, 1985; Tronick, 1989; Tronick & Weinberg, 1997.

9. Chu, 2000; Gilligan, 2003; Pollack, 1998, 2000; Way 1998; Way & Chu, 2004.

10. Brown, 1998, 2003; Brown & Gilligan, 1992; Tolman, 2002.

11. Miller & Stiver, 1997, p. 22.

12. Many thanks to the participants in my Fall 2003 doctoral seminar "Relational Context of Teaching and Learning" for this insight.

13. Miller & Stiver, 1997.

14. Gilligan, 2003, p. 169.

15. Greene, 1973. Thanks to Carol Rodgers for directing me to Greene's terminology of presence.

16. Gilligan, 2004, p. 105.

17. Dewey, 1938/1963, p. 44. Many thanks to Carol Rodgers for pointing me to this passage.

18. Harriet Cuffaro, personal correspondence, December 1, 2003.

19. Dewey, 1910/1933.

20. Dewey, 1910/1933, p. 140.

21. Damasio, 1999.

22. Cuffaro, 1995; Dewey, 1910/1933, 1916/1966; Malaguzzi, 1993; Rodgers, 2002a.

23. Gilligan, 1996; Kegan, 1982; Miller, 1986; Stern, 1985; Surrey, 1991.

24. Pianta, 1999.

25. Brown & Gilligan, 1992; Chu, 2000; Gilligan, 2003.

26. Dewey, 1916/1966, p. 192.

27. Noddings, 2003.

28. Noddings, 2003, p. 172.

29. Cuffaro, 1995, p. 24.

30. Dewey, 1916/1966.

31. Duckworth, 1987; Piaget, 1952/1963; Rogoff, 1990; Vygotsky, 1978; Wertsch, 1985.

32. See, for example, Schunk & Zimmerman, 1997.

33. Belenky, Clinchy, Goldberger, & Tarule, 1986; Gilligan, 1993, 1996, 2003a; Goldberger, Tarule, Clinchy, & Belenky, 1996; Jordan, 1995; Miller, 1986.

34. Gilligan, 1993, 1996, 2003.

35. Winnicott, 1965; Stern, 1985; Trevarthen, 1979.

36. Tronick & Weinberg, 1997.

37. Tronick, 1989.

38. Gilligan, 2003; Chu, 2000.

39. Brown & Gilligan, 1992; Gilligan, 1996; Gilligan, Rogers, & Noel, 1992; Taylor, Gilligan, & Sullivan, 1995.

40. Brown, 1998; Brown & Gilligan, 1992.

41. Belenky, Clinchy, Goldberger, & Tarule, 1986; Goldberger, Tarule, Clinchy, & Belenky, 1996; Jordan, 1995; Miller, 1986; Ward, 2001.

42. Jordan, 1995; Miller, 1986; Miller & Stiver, 1997; Real, 1998.

43. See Birch & Ladd, 1997; Goodenow, 1992; Lynch & Cicchetti, 1997; Midgley, Feldlaufer, & Eccles, 1989; Pianta, 1999; Roeser, Eccles, & Sameroff, 2000.

44. For example, Ross, Hogabaum-Gray, & Rolheiser, 2002.

45. For example, Lynch & Cicchetti, 1997.

46. See Roeser, Eccles, & Sameroff, 2000.

47. It is important to note that the theoretical orientation of this body of research is often based on the paradigm that identifies maturity as individuation and autonomy. A good example of this is in Birch and Ladd's 1997 article focusing on the teacher-child relationship. In this research, they identify five-year-old students' "dependency" on teachers as a negative quality of relationship.

48. This definition of trust in knowledge and self is derived from the interviews conducted for this study, as well as interviews conducted for related studies. See Raider-Roth, 1995a, 1995b, 1995c, 2004, 2005.

49. Hawkins, 1974.

50. Dewey, 1910/1933, p. 140.

51. Connectedness is a dimension of a teacher's presence. For a more extensive discussion of presence, see Rodgers & Raider-Roth, 2004, and Rodgers, 2002b.

52. See Belenky, Clinchy, Goldberger, & Tarule, 1986; Jordan and others, 1991; Jordan, 1995; Miller, 1986; Miller & Stiver, 1997.

53. Surrey, 1991.

54. Miller and others, 1999, p. 2.

55. Miller & Stiver, 1997, p. 54.

56. Belenky, Clinchy, Goldberger, & Tarule, 1986, p. 227.

57. Jordan, 1991, p. 82.

58. Noddings, 2003.

59. Duckworth, 1987.

60. Duckworth, 1987, pp. 86–87, 96–97.

61. Hawkins, 1973.

62. Hawkins, 1973, p. 9.

63. McDermott, 1977.

64. Towler & Broadfoot, 1992.

65. Raider-Roth and others, 2003; Wilma Waithe, personal correspondence, June 16, 2004; Keely Ball, personal correspondence, June 21, 2004.

Part II

Listening to the Students

2

José

"Response Is the Whole Thing"

I t is a gray March day when I first interview José. We sit in a small, overheated office that has two swivel chairs loved by the students in the school for their fast turns. We crack open the huge window in the office, then test the audio equipment. José is not put off by the tape recorder and enjoys the idea that he is being interviewed and might be quoted in a book.

José sports straight brown hair that hangs long around his neck. His wide eyes reveal an alertness and a jovial quality that accompany his fast-paced talk. With his baggy pants and layers of T-shirt and flannel shirt, José shows that he is keenly aware of teen fashion, wearing the current style comfortably. José is twelve years old and came to the school in second grade, when I was his teacher. As José reminds me in the first interview, his first year at the school was one of adjustment when he worked hard to make new friends and puzzled through the newness of the child-centered and open-ended work that was characteristic of the school. I watch him now as he travels through his classroom with ease, offering quiet and friendly as well as sarcastic comments as he passes. I see how at home he has become in the school.

José sees himself as a musician and practices his electric guitar assiduously. José also prides himself on being an actor and takes his class's theatrical enterprises—currently a production of *The Tempest*—very seriously. Clearly, performance is something José enjoys and values. It is José's affinity for acting and performance that

I find challenging in our discussions. At times, I have difficulty discerning whether he is acting for me or telling me what is really on his mind. Perhaps his acting is a way of telling me his thinking. It was later, when I listened to tape recordings of our discussions, that I was able to see the complexity that was embedded in the drama he presented. When I understood the function of the drama, I could hear the texture of his stories. Only then could I listen to his ideas with a stance that was open enough to hear the fullness of his experience.

Getting "All the Help in the World"

José has much to say on the topic of relationship and much to teach me. From the outset of the first interview, José stakes a clear position: his relationships with his teachers must be grounded in safe and protected dialogue that allow him to ask for help. While this sounds like a simple statement, when José and I unpack it, piece by piece, it is a complex and multilayered relational idea. We attend especially to meaning embedded in the words *safe*, *dialogue*, and *help*. We begin our conversation by discussing what it means to ask for help from his teachers. José explains, using self-assessment work as an example: "It feels like you're just talking to someone who can give you all the help in the world."

In this statement, José helps me begin the journey to see that discussions of self-assessment often reveal central relational tensions inherent in classroom life. The first clue in this regard is his location of audience for this personal schoolwork. He clearly sees the audience for his self-assessment as his teachers rather than himself because they are the people he turns to for help. While teachers call this work "self-assessment," indicating that they conceive of it as an exercise meant to understand his "self" as a learner, José views it as an opportunity for interaction rather than introspection.

I ask José about the term *self-assessment* and question its accuracy, because it seems to me that the term does not reflect the reciprocal nature of the endeavor between student and teacher. José responds:

> It's like you tell them what you think you're good at and . . . they're watching you. They see what you're good at; they see what questions you answered, what questions you answered you get wrong, you get right, and then they take, maybe they take notes or maybe they keep them in their head. And then when you do self-assessment work, they . . . recognize it, and they say, "Well, I saw him in class. He's not bad at that. He's, he's pretty good. We should just help him with it."
>
> And it's basically if you told them that you don't think you're any good and that you don't have any self-esteem for it and . . . you don't think you're worth it and . . . that they shouldn't try. And, uh, then they see you in action, and they said that you're good, you're perfect for it, and you're built for it, and you're made for it, and they help you. So, it's like you're helping yourself to be helped.

In this narrative, José explores the connections between how teachers see him and how he sees himself, and the way that self-assessment forms the intersection between these two visions. His teachers have access to his self-perceptions and in turn share their observations with him. Through this recursive process with his teachers—teachers observe him; he asks for help; teachers provide help and support for his learning; he can take risks in areas that are difficult—he is able to build a vision of his *self*. From this perspective, he believes it is appropriate to call this process "self-assessment." In this discussion of self-assessment, José beautifully describes the dialogic and reciprocal nature of his relationship with his teachers.

José uses our interview space as an opportunity to explain the qualities of dialogue and communication that sustain his relationships with his teacher. A key quality of this dialogue is privacy. José explains that self-assessment is a perfect example of private dialogue, because it is a vehicle for asking his teachers for help in a way that is safe and that does not risk public embarrassment:

> Usually I can't stand up in class and say I don't like math because it is hard to learn and hard to memorize all those facts, and I feel like I really need to work on math. And then that's like, that was like two years ago that we had to do that. I—I—we started learning multiplication facts in third grade, and in fifth grade, I could barely remember them, but finally I did it, with the help of my teachers, through self-assessment work, because I told them I'm not very good on math.

When teachers ask José how he feels about his capacity to learn, he uses this secure venue as a successful way of letting them know. He feels that he cannot expose his struggles in front of his peers, and so he values the intimacy and freedom of the privacy inherent in this interaction with his teachers:

> You're telling the teacher this, and the teacher in turn knows your weaknesses, and then you can just express yourself freely.

José locates a sense of freedom in the private communication with his teachers. This freedom allows him to reveal his weaknesses—an act that can be difficult for a twelve-year-old child. By revealing his weaknesses, he allows his teachers to support him and offer him assistance in these areas of vulnerability.

The freedom he experiences in having a private forum for communication with his teachers is rooted in the reciprocity that he expects from his teachers:

You tell them what you're good at, and they tell you
what they think you're good at, and you can make something out of that. It's like they have the spice and you
have the whole ingredient, and if you put it together, . . .
you have yourself.

With this first of many metaphors, José articulates the purpose of
the give-and-take of dialogue with his teachers—constructing
knowledge of himself. He tells them what he knows about his thinking and his work, and they tell him what they think, and then he
can make something out of that, or create shared knowledge.

It's kind of like a back-and-forth sharing. You say your
strengths, and then they give you suggestions, and then
it's like a . . . like an editor of a book. You write a book
of your future, and they edit it for you and take out the
mistakes.

Using dramatic metaphor, José begins to hammer home his central
message of the interview: that connection with his teachers hinges
on genuine response and attention from teachers. How José views
himself as a learner depends on the communication that occurs with
his teachers. Though he is the author or chef, the teachers play key
support roles in his creation of knowledge.

When I comment that teachers' responses are really important
to him, he replies, in a tone implying that he does not understand
why I do not "get it,"

[Response] is the whole thing. It's like you can't have, uh
. . . you can't really have a, uh . . . painting without a
canvas to paint on or something.

With this powerful metaphor to illustrate the reciprocal nature of
relationship and knowledge constructed in relationship, José makes
it clear that the picture of himself that he constructs in school depends heavily on trust in his teachers to support the canvas.

As José and I enter this phase of our discussions, I realize that I am struggling to keep up with José's "metaphorical mastery," as he calls it. I am entranced and drawn into his thinking. Yet I have the sense that as his language becomes more metaphoric, he is beginning to perform for me. The flood of metaphors and the rapidity of his speech cause me to feel a sense of remove. Days later, when I listen to our discussion on the tape recorder, I want to understand the function of his narrative style. I am keenly aware that the interviews are also relational spaces in which the very dynamics we are talking about in school could be playing themselves out. I begin to understand this distance that I detect when I trace the narrative voices in his account.[1] I listen carefully to the pronoun he uses to describe his own experience of being in relationship with his teacher. I attend to his shift from an "I" voice to a "you" voice that is in dialogue with a "they" voice, the voice of his teachers. I carefully excerpt all the phrases that begin with *I, you,* and *they* and line them up sequentially as if they were lines in a poem. In this way, I listen for the psychological essence of José's thinking—the ways in which the "I" or "you" embodies the sense of self that he brings to the discussion with me. Listening in this way, I create a "voice poem" that reveals one facet of José's internal dialogue about the questions I raise:

I	You	Teacher(s)
I can't stand up		
I don't like		
I feel		
I really need to work		
I—I—we started learning		
I could barely remember		
I did it		
I told them		
I'm not very good		

I	You	Teacher(s)
	you're telling	
		the teacher in turn knows
	your weaknesses	
	you can just express yourself freely	
	you tell them	
	you're good at	
		they tell you
		they think
	you're good at	
	you can make	
		they have the spice
	you have the whole ingredient	
	you put it together	
	you have yourself	
	You say	
	your strengths	
		they give you
	You write	
	your future	
		they edit

In reading this voice poem of José's beliefs about reciprocity and response, I can see the shifting of his voice from personal "I" statements to a more general second-person "you." In the "I" statements, José's voice is unsure. The "I" "can't stand up," needs "to work," can "barely remember," and is "not very good." From this stance, José shifts to a "you" voice that is more sturdy. The "you" can talk "freely," "can make something," "say" his "strengths," and "write" his "future." From the safety of the one-step-removed "you" location, José can find a more certain stance.[2] It is from this safe position that I sense José assuming a more distant voice. By using the metaphors and the "you" voice, he is communicating in a way that he knows will keep me engaged while also sharing his experience in a one-step-removed fashion. In this narrative shift, I can also view a parallel process between his relationship with his teachers and the research relationship. Just as he does in his relationship with his teachers, in which he searches for safety in expression, so too he assumes a safe stance with me.

José's narrative voice begins to shift when he describes the importance of telling his teachers about his strengths, not just his weaknesses. He explains:

> Well, it gives me self-esteem, and uhh—it makes me cocky, but I don't share that. It makes me think, "Oh, yeah, I'm the best guitar player in my class." And, uh, . . . it lets you be aware. Sometimes you don't know what your talents are. And then during school you do it, and you realize you have a strength in it, and you tell the teachers, and then maybe they let you do it more often.

In the articulation of his strengths, José develops awareness. The capacity to let the knowledge surface and say it to listening teachers has important consequences. If the teachers are listening, then they will support this developing knowledge and give him opportunities to use the knowledge—such as acting in a musical or playing guitar in school. The awareness and communication of what he knows, the teachers' response to it, and the active use of that knowledge are the key ingredients in a teacher-student relationship that can help José build trust in his knowledge.

José describes his relationship with his fifth-grade teacher Samuel, which contained all the criteria for a trustworthy relationship:

Samuel was a big actor, too. He, he totally like, he took time to rewrite the script of last year's play. And we were like, and we were always talking about acting and stuff, and my self-assessment work, I wrote that I wanted, I wrote that I wanted to work on drama, and he said, "If you do a good audition, I promise you I'll give you a good part and I will work with you, and you'll become a great actor." And he didn't only focus on that, he focused on my math, and he gave me all those tips, and he wrote down the formulas on the sheet, and he said, "You cut these out, and you put 'em in your folder and tape them there and just leave them there for whenever you need them, you can go look." And, uh, he helped and he, he, he stopped the problem. He stopped where I was and fixed it.

The power of José's relationship with Samuel is embodied in Samuel's capacity to help José in both his academic struggles and his creative passions. In this story, José focuses on the importance of genuine conversations with Samuel. Dialogic words such as "talking," "wrote," and "said" are peppered throughout this story. José uses this story to describe the kind of reciprocity he expects in his relationships with his teachers. This kind of reciprocity includes talking together; feeling free to ask for and secure support for his creative desires; and receiving an authentic response, which includes actions of deep meaning to José such as getting help in his acting, getting a good part, and becoming a great actor. Though all of the actions to help him with his creative aspirations are important, José also needs and expects his teachers to support him academically. In describing the math notes that Samuel helped him to create, José conveys a sense of security or safety net that Samuel helps him construct for himself.

In contrast to his voice in the metaphor section, here José narrates this story in a strong "I" voice:

I	You	We	He
			he totally
			he took time
		we were like	
		we were always talking	
I wrote			
I wanted			
I wrote			
I wanted			
			he said
	"you do good"		
			"I promise"
			"I'll give you"
			"I will work with you"
	"you'll become great"		
			he didn't only focus
			he focused
			he gave me
			he wrote down
			he said
	"you cut these out"		
	"you put 'em"		
	"you can"		
			he helped
			he stopped
			he stopped
I was			
			fixed it

The actions José connects to his "I" statements are potent: repeated actions of "wanted," "wrote." These are words of desire, communication, connection, and action. The voices that respond to the "I"—the "you" and the teacher ("he")—respond in kind to the strength of the I, offering generosity of time and attention, promises of greatness, and solutions to academic struggles. A "we" voice appears, as if to represent the collaboration between the voices. In the end, the "I" voice is attended to and what was in need of repair is "fixed."

I am struck by the power that José perceives his teachers to possess. I think about his statement at the beginning of the interview, that teachers can give him "all the help in the world." Indeed, his story of Samuel communicates this very outlook. I wonder if there was ever a time when his teachers did not respond, and I worry about how José might feel undermined in such a situation. When I ask José whether he can recall an occasion like this, he quickly recounts a time when his third-grade teachers did not carefully read his schoolwork and mistook his paper for that of his classmate Josie. He remembers:

> I had a real problem with that, and I got, I threw a little
> fit, and I said, "You know, you're not helping me."

Here again, José's need for help is of paramount concern, and when help is not forthcoming, he becomes angry. I notice that this is the first time that anger enters the conversation. I understand this anger as a response to a break or rupture in the relationship with his teacher. I also begin to understand "help" as a code word for "relationship." When teachers help him, they are connected and in relationship with him. When they do not help, the connection is broken.

A second concern for José is that teachers need to take *time* to help and to connect. I think back to his story about Samuel and remember that a key aspect was that Samuel "took time" with him. In the mix-up with his paper, he believes that his teachers did not take time, as evidenced by their not reading his name carefully. José describes how he experienced their mistake:

JOSÉ: But, uh, the teachers responded in a way that was like, "Okay that's great. Uh, now I have to go drink my coffee," and it was really, it was really, it was not getting to the point. It was like, "We, we want our paycheck and now we want to leave." Well it's not quite like that but . . .

MIRIAM: But that's how it felt—

JOSÉ: (*interrupts*) They cared, but they didn't care enough. They needed to tell me what I was good at, and they didn't.

With this story, José reveals his sharp capacity to read his teachers' attitudes and detect their attentiveness and availability. He readily understands which teachers are there to offer him "all the help in the world" and which teachers are there to collect their "paycheck." By creating such sharp extremes, José reveals the high stakes he feels are embedded in teachers' connections to him. When teachers are not attentive or genuine, he knows that his learning process is compromised. José's final comment, "They cared, but they didn't care enough," argues that it is not sufficient for teachers just to care. Teachers have to care enough, and the criteria of "enough" is measured by their actions of connection and response. The quality of response is vital because it is in this dialogue that his faith in what he knows about himself as a learner is constructed. If there is no response or an inadequate response, both trust in his teachers and trust in what he knows can be compromised. José's message in the first interview is clear: teachers' responsibility for response is immense.

Keeping Away from Himself

Our second interview occurs on a warm, bright June day. This time we are sitting in the third/fourth grade classroom on a comfortable old couch, informally covered by a cotton tan and black print bedspread. In this interview, José and I examine a self-assessment record of his final project, a study of "Metropolis" (a pseudonym for a city in the vicinity of the school). I am hoping in this interview to set the stage for a conversation in which we can talk about the nuances of how this way of communicating with his teachers may or may not have helped him learn. During the first half hour, just as I begin to worry that my questions are not engaging José, he interrupts me to point out a part of this self-assessment work that he thought was not helpful to him. I listen carefully to what he is about to say, because I know that when children interrupt in an interview, they are often trying to tell me what is really on their mind. Picking up his Metropolis self-assessment work, he points to question 14 and to his corresponding response:

> *Question 14: Do you think your work on the [Metropolis] Project offers insight into your personality?*
>
> No, and yes. You can tell me. My aggressiveness shows in my style.[3]

I am fascinated by his written response. I am struck by his bold clarity in voicing his need to hear his teachers' perceptions of his work. I am also startled by his use of the word "aggressiveness" and his sense that this quality shows in his work. I am curious about why he thinks this question is unhelpful. He explains:

> I think that it's wrong that they put that in there 'cause I got sidetracked. I started thinking about myself, not the project, when I wrote that.

With this forceful statement, José begins to discuss with me how thinking about himself can get in the way of thinking about his work. I can see from José's gaze and his stiffened body that he is not performing for me and that we have entered tender territory. I know that I need to tread carefully and respond well. I shift my position on the couch, tucking my feet under me and watching José's pensive face.

I am interested in understanding whether this kind of question can be so provocative as to cause him to lose track of what he

knows about his work. I ask José how he came up with the word
aggressive to describe his style. I wonder if these are his words or
words he has heard from others. He replies:

> I'm telling you the truth that I've heard from others. I've
> heard from myself and I've agreed to. . . . I don't really
> know *if* I'm picky; I don't really know *if* I'm aggressive,
> but other people say "Oh, you're always ticked off." And
> you know, "Oh, you're so picky. Stop it." And I say, "I am
> picky, so deal with it."

He is struggling to disentangle his own beliefs from those of others
that he has incorporated into his belief system. He has heard these
words used about him, and he has agreed to them. The definition
seems to fit. I ask him whether he really believes these words about
himself. In powerful language that feels consistent with his flair for
the dramatic, he explains:

> Well, it began as I got picky in class or I got aggressive
> in class, and then I'd say no, and then I'd go home, and
> it would happen at home when no kids were around. It's
> like, I'd drop something on the floor, oh man! Yeh! And
> then like, uh, I'd go nuts, and I'd pick it up or, uh, I'd be
> hungry, so I'd go, "Yeah, I'M HUNGRY!" or I'd be tired,
> so I'd go straight off to bed no matter what. . . . So I
> think that everything fits together to make me, and
> nothing is really wrong with me. It's just some things,
> sometimes things blow over, and I go nuts. I think every-
> body has to go nuts.

With these examples, José can identify both experiences with other
children and incidents that happen when he is by himself in which
he feels that he loses control over his reactions and emotions. The
feedback he receives from his peers as well as from himself con-
tributes to his sense of self as "aggressive" and "picky." He struggles

to figure out whether his reaction of "going nuts" is extreme or the kind that everybody experiences.

He adds to his powerful description by adding what it means to blow up at school:

> It's like a piece of dynamite that says "pickiness," and it's like I carry it around in my pocket all day, and when I go nuts, I light it and it blows up everywhere. It bounces off the walls and goes into people. It goes around people. People see it, and people get mad at me.

This image is so potent that I understand why José says that thinking about his personality might derail him from thinking about his work. If thinking about himself could cause him to lose control and "blow up," then indeed it most likely feels safer not to think about himself. José's discussion of his explosiveness is honest and clear. I think about the scholarly and practitioner research on boys' anger, aggressiveness, and volatility in school and wonder how the relational dynamics of school contribute to this phenomenon.[4]

While José brings metaphorical language back into the conversation, he sticks closely to the "I" voice. While there is vulnerability in this explosive image, José does not step away from it.

I	It	People
	It's like a piece of dynamite	
	it's like	
I carry it		
my pocket		
I go nuts		
I light it		
	it blows up	
	It bounces	
	It goes around	
		People see it
		people get mad

As José tries to understand the nature of the "it"—"aggressiveness," "pickiness," "going nuts"—the "I" begins from a position of control. The "I" carries and lights "it." "It" then explodes wildly. "It" is forceful and can be hurtful to others and ultimately to José. I am struck that even the physical shape of this voice poem portrays an explosion. The poem is rooted with a strong "I" core, while the "it" lines both above and below the "I" voice are dynamite, blowing up, bouncing, and going around. The explosion tapers off, like the end of a fireworks burst, with fragments of the "they" voice—people seeing José explode and getting angry. I understand this I-it dialogue as José's attempt at portraying how parts of himself (in this case his anger) affect his relationships with his teachers and peers at school. I am paying attention to his description of relationships because he has already described how the quality of these relationships builds his sense of himself as a learner. Although José identifies these aspects of his personality as ones that can "sidetrack" him from thinking about his work, perhaps these are also the very aspects that can derail his relationships.

When I reflect back to José that it sounds like he works hard to control the dynamite, he describes the struggle:

> It's like I keep away from myself when I'm writing my paper to keep me from going nuts. . . . So I keep from myself what I know is not a problem. But it's, uh, something that I didn't do on purpose, but I know what I did wrong, and I know I can fix it. So something I would write down [on my self-assessment] is something that I need help with.

José is describing how he disconnects from knowledge about himself in order to focus on his work. He keeps away from himself or disconnects from his feelings about mistakes that he knows he can solve on his own. He knows that these feelings could trigger him to lose control, go nuts, or become very frustrated with himself. I am fascinated by the notion that in order to help himself, he needs to "keep away" from himself. Interestingly, he stays connected to the larger "problems" in order to gather resources for the situations in which he cannot help himself and in which he needs help to defuse the trigger that this state of vulnerability creates. I want to understand the difference between the kinds of mistakes that he can handle on his own and therefore keep away from himself and those that he needs help with.

I ask José about the relationship between asking for help and "going nuts."

> Going nuts is something when I can't have help and I need help . . . and then so I write down what I will go nuts about, and they stop it from going nuts. So they take away the dynamite, and, uh, they . . . it's, uh, so I write down what I'm picky and what I'm aggressive about and what I eventually will go nuts about, and then they correct it, and then it's all gone, and then I'm back to the unexploded pickiness and aggressiveness that's, uh, waiting for another mistake.

When talking about needing help, José leaves behind the notion of staying away from himself and zeroes in on the kind of help and connection he needs. José believes that when he needs help and cannot have it, he will "go nuts." Again, as in the first interview, "help" appears to be a code for "relationship." In a sense, he is saying that when he is most in need of connection with his teachers and the connection does not happen, he becomes angry and vulnerable. The emphasis he places on reliable psychological and intellectual connection with his teachers is forceful. Connection is a necessary precondition for his learning; the consequences of a loss in relationship are explosive. José believes that if he can ask for help and if his teachers offer genuine response and help, they can help defuse the explosive feelings that accompany the vulnerability he can experience in school. Here again, I more clearly understand how

José experiences his teachers as being able to offer "all the help in the world."

I understand José's volatile imagery in two ways. On one hand, José's sense of control over what he knows is fragile. In the best of times—when he is actively supported by his teachers—he is an un-exploded package that is in danger of confronting a mistake or a place where he feels that his knowledge is shaky. On the other hand, José has a solid system for asking for the kind of help he needs in order to regain equilibrium. When I look at this passage through the lens of the speaking voices, the latter understanding comes through more powerfully:

I	They
I can't have help	
I need help	
I write	
I will go nuts	
	they stop it
	they take away the dynamite
I write down	
I'm picky	
I'm aggressive	
I eventually will go nuts	
	they correct it
I'm back	

Listening in this way, I can see the dyadic nature of José's learning. He asks for help; his teachers defuse the dynamite. He writes down his places of fragility; his teachers support him. His final statement, "I'm back," speaks volumes about the prevailing "I" in this narrative. He does feel that his teachers help him develop his sense of self as a student and as a knower, and he holds on to the notion that they are all-powerful. Yet I think back to his comment from the first interview: "It's like they have the spice and you have the whole ingredient, and if you put it together, . . . you have yourself." He knows he is the whole being and his teachers are the support. He knows that being himself means that he needs the help of the adults in his world. Not only does he build his knowledge about himself as a learner with his teachers, but he also builds a complex system of asking for help to avert what he later terms "havoc," emotional havoc. By having a safe place to ask for help, he can garner the support he needs to manage places of real vulnerability in his schoolwork. The times when he can "go nuts" are the times when he does not trust what he knows or does not know. These are the very times when he wants to ask for help, to build the knowledge and the solidness of his trust in his capacity to know and perform.

Thinking About José

José's stories support many of the cognitive theorists—for example, Piaget, Vygotsky, Rogoff, Schunk, and Zimmerman—in regard to the social construction of knowledge. Indeed, Dewey's notions of interaction and communication are readily apparent. In interaction, knowledge is formed. In communication, knowledge is developed and then internalized or appropriated. But there is another dimension to José's thinking—a relational dimension.

What I learn first from José is that the dynamics of his classroom relationships are key to his capacity to *say* what he does and does not know in school. If he cannot talk and converse, José's sense of himself as a knower is compromised. Second, if he shares the more tender aspects of what he knows, he requires and demands a genuine response from his teachers. The response helps him construct an awareness of what he knows and can help diffuse the strong emotions he experiences when confronted with knowledge that is unsteady. In the context of trusting relationships with his teachers, he can begin to build knowledge that is robust and trustworthy.

José's story about "staying away" from himself raises provocative questions about teachers' attempts to help students "know" themselves and how these efforts can help him construct knowledge that he can trust. José was distressed when the Metropolis self-assessment "sidetracked" him by making him think about his "aggressive" personality rather than his work. From one perspective, we can see this disconnection as adaptive: it allows him to be creative and complete his schoolwork—in this case, the self-assessment work. When he is "sidetracked," his thinking about his work is undermined. José believes that thinking about his temperament, emotional style, and relationships in school will interrupt his engagement with his work.

Paradoxically, it is his very depth of knowledge about his relational style that allows him to use communicative venues such as self-assessment work in a supportive and effective fashion. While there are often good or adaptive reasons for José to "keep away" from himself or from his teachers, there are often concurrent reasons to connect and share ideas and thoughts with his teachers. The complexity of the reciprocal communication that José craves is this very push-pull process of connecting and disconnecting. His powerful desire to disconnect from the feelings related to his vulnerabilities helps him maintain his connection with his work. Simultaneously, his need to connect with his teachers in order to contend with the most difficult challenges and to resolve the associated unsettling feelings is equally potent. With astute intellectual skill, vibrant humor, and sharp relational understandings, José has learned to negotiate this connection dance.

The lingering questions from this encounter focus on the costs of this dance. Is the disconnection that José describes akin to the dissociative process Carol Gilligan identified in the relational development of adolescent girls, which she called a "brilliant but costly solution"?[5] What knowledge about his thinking does José risk losing by "keeping away" from himself? Similarly, what knowledge about his schoolwork did he feel was at risk by being sidetracked and thinking about his personality? I wonder about the dynamics of classroom relationships that can support students' healthy relationships with self—the dynamics that can diminish children's need to disconnect from self and facilitate their capacity to connect with self and others.

José clearly articulates that responsiveness, authenticity, reciprocity, dialogue, safety, and time are key factors of trustworthy relationships with his teachers. Using "help" as his code word, he tells us that the cost of being out of relationship with his teachers is high; it can lead to anger, vulnerability, and, most frighteningly for José, "going nuts" or explosively losing control. His comments make me pause to consider how we think about children's (especially boys') anger and acting out in school. We often interpret it as lack of control, lack of obedience, lack of respect, or lack of a certain biochemical balance. While these factors might account for some behaviors, have we considered the relational factor? When children act out, misbehave, or test limits, perhaps they are telling us that they detect a break in relationship in their classroom, that they no longer feel the essential qualities that José has described. There is much to be learned about classroom life if we think of children's behavior as a barometer of relationship.

Notes

1. A key aspect of the Listening Guide is the second listening (the listening for self), in which close attention is paid to ways that the interviewees speak of themselves in the first-person "I" voice. Similarly important is listening to shifts in that voice to "you" or even "he" or "she." One important way to listen for the voice of self is to extract, in succession, all "I" phrases ("I" plus associated verb) and list them in order. This creates an "I poem" and allows the researcher to hear the ways that the voice of the self speaks in the interview and in relation to the questions being asked. At times, listening to the "I" voice in conversation with the "you" voice allows the researcher to hear the internal conversations that the

interviewee may bring to the discussion. For a more detailed discussion of the second listening, see the Appendix and Gilligan, Spencer, Weinberg, & Bertsch, 2003.

2. The notion of the "you" voice as a distancing move in narrative is well documented in the literature on this voice-centered method (see Brown & Gilligan, 1992).

3. Spelling and mechanics from the original have been preserved.

4. See Gilbert & Gilbert, 1998 and Browne & Fletcher, 1995.

5. Gilligan, 1996, p. 244.

3

Maya

Two Shelves for Knowing

Maya bounds into the small office where we are to sit together. She is ready for our conversation and excited about the interview. On this bright May day, sunlight pours through the big glass window as if to mirror Maya's exuberant energy. She likes the idea of being tape-recorded and expresses visible pleasure in the idea that her words might be included in a published work. When I ask during the interview whether she is getting tired and wants to stop, she replies with a giggle, "I can stay here all day. I love talking about myself."

Sitting attentively in the black swivel chair, Maya is wearing denim shorts and a navy tank top. With her thick, reddish-brown, curly, shoulder-length hair pulled into a tight ponytail, her brown eyes look bigger against her olive skin than I remember. Her summer attire reveals thin, tightly wound, muscular arms and legs. She begins her interview with a detailed account of her role in the schoolwide production of *The Magic Flute*. At age twelve, Maya declares herself a musician and relishes public performance of many kinds. I have vivid memories of Maya at age seven, proudly playing her cello and piano during our music groups at school. Now Maya speaks about her music as an integral part of her life, as a way in which she has come to know the world.

The Tensions of Relationship: Sensing the Pressure

Maya constructs a compelling and complex message throughout our interviews that describes the inherent connection between trusting relationships and her capacity to know what she knows. She explains, with sharp imagery, that in the context of trusting learning relationships, she is able to connect to her knowledge of herself and her work—even the most fragile and discomfiting kinds of knowing. When those relationships become unsafe or lack trust, she may disconnect or dissociate from what she knows. The consequences of this disconnection can be dramatic, and her learning may be compromised.

I launch our discussion with a question about her opinion of self-assessment work. This proves an important starting point, for the conversation soon focuses on the ways that her teachers' perceptions of her learning capacities can apply great pressure on her own self-perceptions. Maya is eager to talk about this work and begins by telling me that she likes self-assessment because "you can say what you truly think." She enjoys having a place in which she can talk to herself about her projects and her work. Self-reflective tasks come easily to her because she knows where she excels and enjoys writing and talking about these qualities.

She is clear, however, that the self-reflective and self-disclosing acts that accompany self-assessment work serve not only a pleasurable purpose but also a clear political purpose. Though Maya is a strong student and excels academically, she worries that her teachers can be critical of her performance. She appreciates opportunities to reveal a "true" picture of herself.

> I think [self-assessment] is cool because that it's like you
> get to grade yourself almost. Because when teachers do
> it, it's always a feeling of like, umm—that like, "Oh gosh,
> I didn't do this right," you know, I have to do it again

because they said it wasn't great enough and I got this question wrong. When you get to do it, you can, you want to just ask you how you think you were writing in school; you can say what you truly think, which I like. Otherwise, if the teachers just said your writing on a re-port card or something and is, you know, below average, you're not like you're not good at nonfiction, you're da ta da ta da, it gives you more low self-esteem. So you need to write about yourself.

Maya suggests here that the opportunities for discussion of "self" and learning, especially written ones, can be self-protective in that they can counter critique from her teachers, which can have the severe effect of "low self-esteem." Maya is especially attuned to issues of critique because she has reacted strongly to one of her sixth-grade teachers, Vicki, who resigned shortly before this re-search began. Maya felt that Vicki was highly critical of her and her classmates, was quick to anger, did not understand her aca-demic needs, and, most disturbingly, did not understand how Maya felt. She recounts that once when she was telling Vicki that she needed more challenging schoolwork, Vicki responded to Maya and her classmates that they were "too proud of themselves." Maya re-flected on that experience by saying that that was "not at all what we were feeling." Maya's response to this kind of critique and to her relationship with Vicki became more central as our conversa-tions continued.

Our conversation quickly became focused on experiences in which Maya and her teachers held divergent opinions about her knowledge and performance. She referred to her fifth-grade teach-ers, who "seemed to think that I was behind in math," and so "I was like, 'I'm not good at math.'" This year, however, her teachers placed Maya in the "harder math groups," and now she thinks she is "actually good at math."

When I ask her what changed between last year and this one, she explains that her teacher last year "told me I wasn't good at math." I press her on this point and ask her if he really told her she was not good at math. With this question, she explains her way of reading her teachers' intentions and how she could sense what he thought:

> He didn't tell me that, but you could sense that that's what he thought. He took kids that . . . they didn't understand this stuff, to work on it, to understand it, even though I knew it perfectly well.

Though her teacher didn't tell her in words, she knew what he thought by virtue of the kind of work he assigned and the alignment between the work and her needs as a student.

Maya returns to this story in the second interview and expands on the pressure she experienced from negative assessment of her skills and knowledge. She contrasts this experience with one in which the teachers accurately assessed what she knew:

> I mean, actually it kept being pushed on me so much I actually did think I wasn't good at math, but then totally as soon as he got switched to teach the sixth graders and the other teacher came to teach the fifth graders, I was fine again because I got everything totally right, and it was like I knew what to do and it wasn't going to take me fifty years to figure out this problem.

Following the "I" voice in this narrative, I see that Maya's connection to her knowledge begins at a shaky point; she feels the teacher's perceptions were pushed on her, and she says, "I did think I wasn't good." Her relationship to her knowledge changes when a new teacher steps in; after that, Maya says, "I was fine," "I got everything," and "I knew." The sharp distinction between feeling stressed and unsure and feeling confident and knowledgeable is painfully clear and is directly linked to the quality of Maya's connection with the different teachers.

In these stories, Maya recognizes that when teachers doubt her capacities and impose their perspectives on her, she too begins to doubt her own abilities. She astutely reads her teachers' cues, and even though her fifth-grade teacher did not say that she was a poor math student, she could "sense" his thoughts through his actions, like placing her in a lower math group. Yet at the same time that Maya doubts her abilities, she believes that she knows the math and asserts that the teacher placed her in a lower group "even though I knew it perfectly well." I am sensing that while Maya's teachers' perceptions of her can undermine her trust in herself, they do not undermine what she actually knows.

However, there is a different kind of pressure that seems to have a more undermining effect. Maya returns to the notion of pressure when I ask her if she has ever worried about the veracity of her writing in her self-assessment work.

> Sometimes . . . you feel all this pressure to say what you are not good at. 'Cause they're always saying, "What are your strengths in this? What are your weaknesses?" And there is always a strength, and [*talking very fast*] I'm sure there's always a weakness and, but what you're saying, sometimes you just have to—it's just almost, sometimes it's almost pressuring you to think of what you're not good at and to think of what you are good at.
>
> So I've always—I mean I have—personally, I do have a lot of self-esteem, so I'm always writing the stuff that I'm good at. And [*pause*] things that I'm not good at, there's always something that I write about, definitely. And then I'm like, wracking my brain and thinking, well, I have to write something, so I'm going to say that I'm not good at this. When you never know if it's true,

and even with the things that I am good at, and you
never know if that's true either.

Maya's response focuses on questions that ask students to identify
their strengths and weaknesses (for example, "What do you think
you are best at?" "What work is most challenging for you?"). In both
her interviews, Maya often talks about these kinds of questions
because for her, they are fundamental features of the self-assessing
process. In this response, Maya explains that locating her strengths
comes easily for her because "I do have a lot of self-esteem." She
feels pressure from "them"—presumably her teachers—however, to
articulate an academic weakness and admit what is difficult for her.
Assessing this aspect of knowing is complicated for her, and the
struggle raises questions about the veracity of her writing. When she
begins to have difficulty articulating what she knows, she then
doubts the truthfulness of her knowledge about her strengths. The
sense of pressure that she experiences from her teachers does not
help her construct knowledge or articulate her struggles. This narrative suggests that the pressure to examine areas of struggle can
push her to doubt what she knows.

The Meaning of Strengths and Weaknesses:
The World of Shades and Shelves

In thinking about the kinds of pressure that Maya experiences in
school, I find myself focusing on her comments about self-esteem.
There is the refrain of having "a lot of self-esteem" that returns
throughout the interview. Her opening discussion of self-assessment
also described the "low self-esteem" that can result from teacher critique. I begin the second interview directly by asking Maya what it
means to "have a lot of self-esteem," a term I am struggling to
understand. I want to unpack factors that help Maya hold on to
what she knows and the forces that cause her to lose hold of her
knowledge. Maya eloquently explains the concept of self-esteem:

To know that you are not the lowest form, the lowest life form on earth. [*laughs nervously*] Umm—and that you are here for a purpose and that you, umm—and that you are good at things and that you realize that what you are good at and what you are not, and how you know, like, you're there for a reason and everything. And umm, and that, I don't know, I mean it's like, it's nice to know that I can play the cello and the piano 'cause I always have something that I can look at that I know I'm good at.

I am struck by her notion that having a lot of self-esteem is connected to her feeling that her life has a purpose and to her sense of competence and capability. For Maya, being "there for a reason" is intimately linked with being "good at" playing the cello and piano. She reiterates this connection when I ask her how she thinks this self-esteem came about:

I was born with it. [*laughs*] Um, my parents just made me that way, I guess? That I was here for a good reason. And not that I was just some crappy old thing put here for no—that like, you know, I kind of grew up just setting my mind I'm gonna play cello and I'm starting in the fall and get me lessons and like, I knew.

Her sense of self-esteem is intimately bound up with a feeling that she exists for a purpose. As she continues to explain self-esteem, she describes how she learned to play the cello when she was seven. She told her parents, "I want cello lessons, and I'm starting in the fall." She explains that she chose the cello because "It was kind of like I knew what I wanted because I knew I'd be good at it."

I ask Maya how she knew that she would be good at the cello, and she recounts the "exact date" that she was lying on her parents' bed and decided, "Okay, I'm going to start the cello now." She knew her mom loved the cello, and she thought, "Why don't I play the cello for her?" I comment that it sounds like she made the decision for her mother. She replies,

> I think I thought about that when I decided, but then when I . . . I did it for myself. And then when I started it, you know, I wanted to play it the minute I got home. I just like sat down and like, "Look, I can play 'Twinkle, Twinkle [Little Star]' on this, this one string." And it wasn't like I could play; it was just like I could do that on the first day. I knew how to hold the bow, and I was so proud of myself and everything that day.

As I listen, I hear her sense of finding a piece of herself when she began to play the cello. This story illuminates both her bond with her mother and the ways that this relationship is linked to her feelings of competence. When I listen to this story through her "I voice," I hear the strength and animation that Maya expresses about her knowledge. I can feel her confidence and excitement:

I think

I thought

I decided

I did it for myself

I started

I wanted

I got home

I just sat

I can play

I could play

I could do

I knew how

I was so proud of myself

The "I" voice is solid in telling this story. Through the "I" lens, Maya uses language of knowledge, action, desire, pride, and confidence. Her sense of knowledge appears internally bound. Yet her relationship with her mother, her primary teacher, figures largely in the story. I am reminded of the shift in her narrative voice when she described the math teacher with whom she felt connected. Her sense of knowledge became more robust, more confident. Clearly, from Maya's perspective, the relationships with those who teach her help to shape her experience of trust in what she knows.

I also sense that the subject matter, the "it" as defined by David Hawkins,[1] or the focus of study within the teaching-learning relationship, shapes Maya's relationship with her knowledge. When Maya is in relationship with her cello and music, her knowledge is most robust. When Maya is connected to her greatest strength, she can rely on the knowledge within.

Seeing the security of Maya's knowledge in this context, I am interested in how she relates to the knowledge that she feels is weaker. I think about Maya's earlier comment that she feels pressured to admit her weaknesses and the consequent disconnection from knowledge. When I ask her about this difficulty, she replies:

> [in a quiet voice] I can't say. Something unconscious, because . . . maybe I grew up in such a world that it really . . . never occurred to me to think about the things that I was really bad at. You know? . . . I think it's because that I'm so unused to thinking about my weaknesses in school and stuff. I just can't do it—I'm just so unused to thinking about it.

Maya's struggle with this way of thinking about her work is evident. When listening to her narrative through the first-person voice, her struggle to know her areas of weakness is vivid:

I can't say

I grew up

I was really bad

I think

I'm so unused to thinking about my weaknesses

I just can't do it

I'm just so unused to thinking about it.

When considering her knowledge through the lens of weakness, Maya cannot think or speak: "I can't say. . . . I'm so unused to thinking. . . . I'm just so unused to thinking." Her capacity to know herself in this context is clearly challenged. Her difficulty here mirrors the difficulty she experiences when she feels pressure from her teachers to recognize weakness.

Maya's portrayal of the disparate worlds of strengths and weaknesses is fascinating. She draws them distinctly and separately. In the arena of "a lot of self-esteem," where she is connected to trusting teachers and others, she is articulate, energetic, reflective, and thoughtful. In the world of weaknesses, there is a sense of solitude, and she is quieter, having difficulty accessing her thoughts and finding the words to say what she knows. This discrepancy is important, because it sheds light on the essential features that help her connect with what she knows.

As we try to disentangle this tension, I remember that earlier in the interview, when Maya talked about aspects of self-assessment work that she does not like, she pointed to the questions that ask her to reflect on work that was easy or challenging. "I can't always answer those," she stated. She resisted the artificial separation or dichotomy:

It's usually balanced, like easy and challenging, and it's kind of like you're both there in everything, in every aspect. It's not like the whole entire thing, it's not like one part was really hard and one part was really easy. Usually if I know if it's balanced, I'll know I did good work on it, because I know it was the perfect level.

Maya was saying that it was hard for her to separate her work into "easy" and "challenging" categories because she could see both aspects in her work. It is her comment "it's kind of like you're both there in everything, in every aspect" that I am remembering as I hear her struggle to talk and think about weakness. I am struck by the phenomenon that in some instances she can see strengths and weaknesses, but when asked to think only about weaknesses, she struggles.

I remind her of her earlier thoughts on the unity of strengths and weaknesses and ask her how it relates to her current ideas that thinking about weakness is difficult. I also notice and point out that she has written about this idea of unity in her sixth-grade end-of-the-year self-assessment. We read the following excerpts together:

> *Question 10: What do you think your greatest strength was this year?*
>
> My strengths pretty much all melted in the first part of the year. And when the second half came, my strengths came back together and were solid again. As I said, in everything I have had some strengths and weaknesses.

Yet, in response to the next question about weakness, she wrote:

> *Question 11: What do you think your greatest weakness was this year?*
>
> In the beginning of the year I just felt plain weak. After the [Metropolis] Project my only weakness was . . . (I can't think of one).

In these two responses, she demonstrates the very tension I noticed previously. I point out to Maya that she seems to believe that everything has a strength and a weakness, yet when asked only about weakness, she has difficulty locating this aspect of her learning. As soon as I say this, her eyes widen and a slow smile spreads across her face. She responds with a new animation in her voice:

> Yes, it's true. Umm, like yeah, 'cause as I say here everything has both. . . . If I think about it that way, I could probably pick out all my weaknesses in the cello.

Maya then explains about a very difficult thumb position on the cello and her struggle to shift into this position when she is playing. As I watch her excitement in telling me about this difficulty, I tell her that it seems that she has just figured out a new idea. I ask her what she means by "if I think about it that way." She responds:

> I didn't realize I answered this question that way. When I think that everything is exactly even and that everything has a—and that every two aspects or both the aspects of my life, strengths and weaknesses, I can pick out both. I can pick it all out.

Maya has realized that while before she did not understand the meaning of her response in her end-of-the-year self-assessment, she now knows what she meant when she said "in everything I have had some strengths and weaknesses." She realizes that if she uses a place of strength, such as her cello, as the foundation for looking at the places in which she feels less secure, she can see what she could not see before.

I tell Maya that I want to understand how she was able to make that move. I am amazed that I have been able to witness this coming to know, or making of connections, right before my eyes. I think about how, in the first interview, Maya had described knowing what she knows as a "clicking" experience: "As soon as it clicks, I always find the clicking moment in everything. Like, I didn't get it, and then finally I'm like, 'Oh! Obviously!'"

I now tell her that I feel as if I had just seen her have a "clicking" experience and ask her to explain what happened. She explains that she wrote the answers on the self-assessment sheet "unconsciously" and did not "really read it over." Now, as Maya reads it again, "I can see what I actually meant when I said that. It's just kind of like my hand just wrote it?" She articulates her learning clearly:

> When I realized that the two divided halves in your life both have—well, I was thinking about it in a big picture, like one is your strength and one is your weaknesses. And when then I realized your weakness half also has strengths in it and your strength also has weaknesses in it, and you can try to pick out little things in it. . . .
> The challenging picture was more clear in my head. I was kind of like, totally in my head just like, wah, like confused, like messed up, like everything was like a total blur, but now I realize I can see the two little halves.

As Maya is able to connect her knowledge of strengths with her knowledge of weakness, she is able to create a new sense of knowing that is complete and embodied. The vision images are particularly potent. She can now see what her hand wrote: "I can see what I actually meant," "everything was like a total blur," "I can see the two little halves." As she comes to know a piece of herself, she is able to see aspects of her thinking that she had not seen before. She is surprised and amazed that she had written about having the idea that each area of her life has strengths and weaknesses. Yet in the context of this conversation, she realized the meaning of what she "actually meant." When I listen to this narrative through the "I" voice, Maya's connections to her knowledge are amplified:

I	*You*
I realized	
	your life
I was thinking	
	your strength
	your weaknesses
I realized	
	your weakness
	your strength
	you can try
I was	
I realize	
I can see	

Representing her internal dialogue, the "you" and "I" voices converse about her process of coming to know. In this dialogue, the "you" brings reassurance and unity to living with both strengths and weaknesses and invites the "I" to try to think about herself in this totality. The "I" begins to see what she had not seen before. What was unconscious before is now conscious.

As Maya and I enjoy these moments of learning and realization, I venture back to the world that is less comfortable. I return to the question of not being able to think about weaknesses. I am curious whether her recent realization will help her to reach a part of her knowledge that feels off-limits. I am stunned when, all of a sudden, she is able to locate this knowledge. She begins by describing the images that hold her back and articulately explains why she could not talk or think about the weaknesses:

I blocked it out. I live consciously in a place closer to the strengths.

I marvel at her astute reading of her own psychological processes. Maya has access to and now locates words to describe how she reads and interprets her psychic experiences. Maya reveals the extent of her insight when she describes the forces that separate the strengths and weaknesses:

> When I read what my own body wrote I can just see [*we both laugh*] what really *is*. It's kind of like, it kind of like feels like camouflage. It just feels like this whole shade in front of the real thing. I mean, I see this other thing that you created, but then when you see the real big picture, you can pull up the shade and you can see it.

Here she vividly narrates the psychological mechanisms that divide her world of weakness from the world of strengths. I am struck by the images of camouflage and the shade, and her persistent use of visual actions to symbolize what she had come to know: "I see," "you see," "you can see it." Maya uses vibrant language to describe how she has created a shade to keep these worlds separate. When she pulls up the shade and can connect the two parts of her life, she sees what her "own body wrote." She knows that the "real thing" or the wholeness of her knowledge is created when she pulls up the shade and can connect the two parts of her life. She knows both the importance of unifying these pieces of her knowledge and the reality of their separation.

At this juncture, I remember an earlier comment in which she described her life at home, in which she does not think about her weaknesses. I ask her what keeps her away from thinking about weaknesses in that context. This question unleashes a story about a severe illness in Maya's life:

> I was just so sick, and so I couldn't do anything. I felt like an invalid because I just like, couldn't go anywhere without coughing, like stopping, and I was gonna die because I couldn't breathe. And so I couldn't really practice, I

> couldn't go to my piano, and I couldn't do this and
> I couldn't do that. . . . I didn't know what it was like to
> not have it. . . . I didn't know what it was like to be a
> normal person again.

I ask what it was like to be "normal," again and she replies, "Yeah, I felt like who-a-a-! [*laughs*] I'm here again!" She continues to describe the difference between being sick and normal with another astute metaphor:

> It was like two separate shelves. You got one thing on
> this shelf that's the, that's the horrible stuff, and then
> your life becomes this other shelf, and you just like, put
> the other stuff on the other shelf, and you just get rid of
> it, and you just—I don't even think of it as part of my
> life anymore.

In asking her to consider a context in which she does not think about weaknesses, she tells a story of illness in which her weakness is most pronounced. In this poignant description of her illness, Maya describes in magnificent detail the psychological process of dissociation, or disconnecting from that which is most painful. In separating out the "stuff" that is "horrible" and not thinking of it as part of her life, she is able to leave that pain behind. She protects herself. However, these "separate shelves" act like the "shade" she described earlier and can prevent her from thinking about her less debilitating weaknesses, thus stopping her from being able to "see the real big picture" of herself.

   I am impressed not only by Maya's capacity to acutely describe the shade, the shelves, and the camouflage but also the psychological strength she has to lift the shade in a way that feels safe and enlightening. I am moved by her capacity to connect to aspects of her thinking that had felt out of reach, so that she can see or know the full spectrum of her knowledge. I can see the function of the separation, which permits her to not think about painful events. But as with José, the consequences of this dissociation is a loss of knowledge of self.

I begin to worry that Maya is tired or stressed from the intensity of making these important connections to areas of vulnerability in her life. I bring us back to what I think is the more benign ground of self-assessment work. I have forgotten that it is the questions about her end-of-the-year sixth-grade self-assessment work that triggered the ideas about the separation and unity of strengths and weaknesses and that it is in this venue that she built new connections. I return to the question of truth in her self-reflective work and ask if she feels she told the truth in the end-of-the-year work. She replies that she thinks so but says "it's hard to tell" because the first part of the year with Vicki was so difficult for her. When she thinks about a book she read during that time, she says, "it stops my brain." I ask Maya what stops her brain. I am struck by the powerful image in her reply:

> Thinking about the beginning of the year, because of it was just so, such a, like, a nothing of a learning atmosphere, so I guess I couldn't think about it.

By asking a question about the truth of her responses, I realize that I am asking her to consider the relational aspects of her self-assessment work. When thinking about the truthfulness of her words, she must consider to whom she is talking and what she feels she can say in that relationship. When Maya contemplates the veracity of her sixth-grade self-assessment, she zeroes in on her relationship with her teachers. She explains that because of the lack of trust in her relationship with Vicki, she has difficulty even thinking about what she learned in the context of this relationship. She cannot even think about the book she read during this time. The idea of thinking about the time when Vicki was her teacher literally "stops" her brain. In this relationship, she cannot think.

Although I have tried to move us away from the fragile world of considering that which has been dissociated, Maya holds us firmly in that place. When I ask her to think about the truth of her self-disclosures, she identifies the classroom interactions that push her to disconnect from what she knows. Living with a teacher whom she could not trust became a force that stopped her from knowing what she knows and undermined her trust in her knowledge. This relationship helped Maya build a shade between what she could know in safe contexts, such as her music, and what she could know and trust in the classroom. Recalling what Maya wrote about her strengths and weaknesses in her sixth-grade self-assessment drives her point home:

> My strengths pretty much all melted in the first part of the year. And when the second half came, my strengths came back together and were solid again. . . . In the beginning of the year I just felt plain weak.

I am impressed by Maya's capacity to put words to and name her understanding of this distressing experience. I am moved by her capacity now to see her own complexity.

Thinking About Maya

Maya and I traversed complicated territory in these discussions. She taught me that the relationship in which she learns provides an essential context for her capacity to see herself fully. In the context of safe and trusting relationships, such as those with her mother or her sixth-grade mathematics teacher, she feels "a lot of self-esteem"; she feels purpose and meaning in her learning. In these contexts, she can "pull up the shade" and see what she knows as well as what she does not know. She can see a multidimensional picture of her knowledge. In short, she can connect to the many ways she knows herself, ideas, and the people around her.

I also learned these lessons from Maya on another level when I examined the relational context of the interview itself. Interviewing Maya was a provocative experience for me. Because Maya identified herself as someone with "a lot of self-esteem"—an experience of herself that differed dramatically from my own recollections of being twelve—I found myself feeling distant, even tuning out, and lacking the tools to understand her internal dialogue about relationship. I realized that I had to work hard to understand what *her* experience was and what those words meant to her. When I began to try to stand in her shoes, I was able to see a fuller picture of Maya. She began to be a multifaceted person, full of rich complexity.

As I moved to a place where I was able to see the complexity of her thinking, Maya began to lift the shade that separated the pieces of her knowledge. Reflecting on the interview as a parallel experience of the teacher-student relationship, I see that there is a pressing issue of learning and teaching to consider here. If I, the interviewer, was having difficulty hearing her words, Maya astutely read my responses and in turn only communicated what she thought I could hear and understand. When my stance changed and I began to ask questions that indicated I could hear her ideas and enter her world, Maya's stories grew more complex. She began to bring more of her self into our conversation. As a result, she was able to make important discoveries and connect to knowledge that had previously been out of reach.

In this experience of parallel process—that is, experiencing in the context of the interview the very dynamic that Maya describes as occurring in the classroom—there is much to be learned. In both Maya's stories and our interaction in the interview, the connection between relationships and her capacity to access her full spectrum of knowledge is evident. When teachers do not see her in her fullness or doubt her strengths, Maya loses her trust in what she knows. She feels as if it "stops" her brain. When I could not hear her internal experience of self-esteem, she could not talk about the meaning of this phenomenon. When she senses that teachers support her strengths and genuinely see her perceptions of her learning, then she can "pull up the shade" and see herself in her wholeness. When I shifted my stance to listen more fully to her story, Maya was able to create new knowledge about herself.

Maya's stories carry a central message for teachers: in order for students to construct knowledge that is trustworthy, teachers must position themselves in a listening and learning stance. They need to be prepared to hear the meaning that students make of their learning, even if that experience is divergent from the teachers' own experiences. For teachers, this stance requires a recognition of self. For me as a researcher, this was true as well. In particular, the listening stance requires a recognition of blind spots, of defended quarters, of places where it is hard to sanction knowledge and experience that diverges from one's own. This act of self-reflection or self-recognition is akin to a "reader's response" in the world of narrative analysis.[2] In a reader's response, the reader locates her reaction to the text in order to recognize the life history and bias that she brings to the text and that colors how she understands what she reads.[3] In doing such self-reflection and locating how he reacts to his primary "text"—the student—a teacher locates what he brings to the relationship. In this act of recognition and inclusion of self, a teacher can distinguish between his own issues and those of the student, allowing him to be more open to hearing a student's perspectives and experiences. Maya teaches us that when teachers become genuinely available to hear students' reading of the relational world, students perceive this stance of openness and are then apt to say what they know more readily. The capacity to articulate what they know creates fertile ground for making new connections and for building new knowledge. In the context of this kind of relationship, knowledge can be trusted.

Notes

1. Hawkins, 1974.

2. Brown & Gilligan, 1992.

3. Gilligan, Spencer, Weinberg, & Bertsch, 2003.

4

Sharon
Constructing Confidence

S haron and I sit down in the music room with awkward ease. While we have experienced the familiarity of walking the school halls together and of knowing each other well, there is a felt awkwardness of not having been together in the school building for four years and of being in a formal interview. I have a close relationship with Sharon and her family; I taught both Sharon and her older brother Jon (the student introduced in the Introduction). I have seen Sharon frequently over the past four years and have watched her turn the corner from childhood to early adolescence. As we sit together, I feel the calmness of her physical presence. I think it is this quality that made her one of the few strangers with whom my infant daughter would engage with smiles rather than tears. Though I try to diminish the formality of the interview, the tape recorder on the table and the notebook and pen at my side remind both of us that our interaction today is unusual.

Sharon is twelve years old, with long, thick honey brown hair that is most often pulled back in a ponytail. With soft brown eyes and a shy smile, Sharon's gaze is quiet yet open, revealing her poised and astute observational stance. When I see her in her sixth-grade classroom, she is most often sitting with one of many friends, writing, chatting, giggling, and easily alternating between focusing on her own work and maintaining comfortable conversations with a friend. Sharon has a tall, athletic build that serves her well in the various athletic challenges she takes on. She enjoys the social camaraderie of sports and explains that it is a good way for her to make new friends. Today, she is wearing loose-fitting satin-sheen navy workout pants, a comfortable black T-shirt, and a delicate royal blue collar-length beaded necklace.

Finding Her Words

Throughout both interviews, Sharon weaves a central thread: the way she reads her relationships with both others and herself is integrally linked with her capacity to say what she knows. In examining the key aspects of relationship that shape how she voices her knowledge, she identifies the issues of audience and confidence as especially salient in saying what she knows. Having been Sharon's teacher, I know that the location of words and voice has been a central developmental task for her. After she graduated from Terrace, Sharon and I looked through a collection of her teachers' narrative reports about her progress. Indeed, Sharon's development of a strong voice with which she could express herself in the classroom was repeatedly noticed and supported throughout her years at the school.

In the interviews, the tone of Sharon's voice reveals her struggle to make herself heard. When she is sure of her responses, she speaks in full thoughts with a bold voice. When she feels unsure of herself or confused about my questions, she speaks softly and in phrases, almost swallowing the last half of her words. I find that I have to ask her to repeat herself, so that I can hear all of her words. Her narrative is sprinkled with the word "like," as if to fill the spots where she is searching for words. She tends to use "like" more frequently when she is struggling to say what is on her mind. Thus, when Sharon stakes the position that classroom relationships help her say what she knows, I take notice. I am interested in hearing how she describes the process of articulating what she knows and how this effort reflects her understandings of the relational world of the classroom.

"Getting It Right": The Essence of Communication

We begin our conversation grounded in the world of self-assessment. Early in the interview, Sharon takes the position that self-assessment does not help her come to know herself. She does, however, see that self-assessment can be useful in helping her communicate:

> In some ways, it helps me communicate [my ideas], like in some ways, so that I can get help with the weaker points and so that I can let people know I don't need help with the stronger points. It just helps me like, find a way to put it that doesn't make myself seem like, "Oh I know this so well I don't need to do that." Or it doesn't make me seem like, "Oh, I don't know anything."

Sharon understands that if she communicates her strengths and weaknesses to her teachers, then they can support her where she needs help and offer freedom where she is feeling strong. She is clear, however, that learning how to communicate these ideas involves figuring out how to modulate her voice so that she is not heard as self-congratulatory or self-deprecatory.

In this response, self-assessment again reveals itself as a clear vantage point onto the relational dynamics of the teacher-student relationship. Seeing self-assessment as a forum for communication between teachers and students, Sharon unearths the complexity inherent in that communication. When I try to understand what she means by "communicating," she explains:

> I just want to communicate it in a way that like, gets the point across, and like, say, well, "My stronger points are this and . . . my weakest points are this." But in a way that doesn't feel like I'm making myself seem so bad or I'm making myself seem like the best at anything like that.

Here she restates her previous concern that communicating involved getting her "point across" in a way that is publicly acceptable. She is aware that others are interpreting her words and their interpretation is dependent on the way she speaks. She emphasizes this point: "It's sort of the *way* I say it or the way that it's interpreted." When I ask who would be interpreting her words, she responds,

> Well, the teachers are like, interpreting it. And I don't want them to interpret it the wrong way, because then they might get like the total wrong ideas of what I think about myself and what I think about my strong points and weak points and that stuff.

Ultimately, she wants to be perceived well by her teachers so that they don't get the "wrong ideas" about her self-perceptions. She places a high premium on teachers getting an accurate understanding of her capacities, and she is clear that the *way* she articulates her knowledge is key in her teacher's interpretations.

I ask her how she knows when her teachers have gotten it right. She responds in a noticeably decided tone of voice:

> How do I know? I know when they've gotten it right when—It's sort of like, in the beginning of the year . . . everyone had . . . like, a big math packet and when you finished that you'd get another one and so on. . . . I knew a lot of the stuff, and I knew that they understood I knew it when, instead of making me do the whole thing, which was really long, they said, "Well, will you try these?" . . . And then when they—like saw that I understood and I knew how to do it, they let me go on, instead of having to stay behind.

Sharon believes that teachers get it "right" when they see her strengths and design her learning opportunities accordingly. In this response, the volume and cadence of her voice mirror the idea she is describing. That is, in describing effective communication—when her teachers "get it right"—Sharon communicates with me in a confident, assured manner, so that I am able to "get it right" as well. She talks with a sense of certainty, answering this question in a bold tone of voice, with each word articulated confidently. Together with her confident manner, the narrative helps me see that in the context of a story in which she feels understood and known, she is able to articulate and communicate what she knows.

This dynamic is illuminated when listening to this story in the first-person voice, which is in active dialogue with the "they" voice. The dialogue highlights the interplay between Sharon's sense of her own knowing and her sense of her teachers' knowledge of her:

I	They (Teachers)
I know	
I know	
	they've gotten it
I knew	
I knew	
	they understood
I knew	
	they said
	they . . . saw
I understood	
I knew	
	they let me go

In this dialogue, the communication of mutual understanding is strong. In the "they" voice, Sharon portrays teachers who understand her and let her know, through what they say, see, and do, that they will let her "go." They will give her the freedom to learn more challenging work. The "I" voice, in response, stands firm in understanding and knowing. Her phrase "I knew" repeats throughout the narrative. In the context of being known by her teachers, Sharon can know herself as well.

"Getting it Wrong": Feeling Misunderstood

In thinking about this story, I want to understand what it would mean to Sharon if her teachers got it "wrong"—if she felt that they did not perceive her accurately. I want to understand how getting it wrong would affect her sense of being able to communicate. She tells another mathematics story in response:

> Umm, in the beginning of the year when I was saying how I like, told my teachers that I knew how to do percentage things, and like, I knew how to find the percent of something. Like in the beginning, I had that packet, and they were like, "Oh, well, why don't you keep going and do these?" And I had to do like—and I was like in the beginning, I had to do the whole packet. And it was really boring, because I knew it. So I was like just sitting there and doing, like it was just boring busywork, and so I felt like they didn't understand that I knew it, and they didn't give me a chance at first.

In this instance, Sharon feels that although she knew the concept of percentages, her teachers had not discovered or trusted this aspect of her knowledge. Though she tells them what she knows, they doubt her knowledge. She feels misunderstood and belabored by their lack of insight. Yet when I listen to this story in the "I" voice, I hear Sharon maintain remarkable strength.

I	They
I was saying	
I like told	
I knew	
I knew	
I had	

I	*They*
	they were like, "Oh, well"
I had to	
I was	
I had to	
I knew it	
I was like just sitting there	
I felt like	
	they didn't understand
I knew it	
	they didn't give me a chance

Just as in her prior narrative about being understood, the "I knew" refrain remains steadfast. She resists her teachers' lack of understanding and, rather than doubt her own capacities, she is solid in her sense of knowing. Yet she inserts the new phrase "I had to" into the narrative, adding an element of obligation or feeling pushed. In addition, the filler word "like" is peppered throughout this response (inserted nine times in comparison to three times in the prior response). Her capacity to articulate what she thinks is challenged, but she holds fast to her ideas. Sharon understands that she was doing the work because of her teachers' perceptions of her rather than her own. She maintains a secure grasp on what she knows and resists the external pressures in order to persist in holding on to this knowledge.

Though Sharon seems to be resilient in the face of teachers who do not see her full capacities, she is clear that her teachers' perceptions of her do have an impact on her. They can offer her opportunities or hold her back. I begin to wonder whether and how their perceptions of her performance shape Sharon's own understandings of her knowledge. That is, in modulating her voice so that she does not appear "so bad" or "the best," does she modulate her knowledge of herself? The interplay between Sharon's perspectives and her teachers' interpretations surfaces as we discuss how the issue of audience relates to work in school.

Finding Her Audience

The concept of audience looms large in our second interview. As we reflect on her self-assessment of the Metropolis Project, I ask Sharon for whom she thinks she was writing this work. She replies:

> My teachers. I mean well, sort of my teachers. But I was sort of writing it for myself so that . . . maybe in a few years or something I would like, come across my [Metropolis] brochure I might be like, "Oh yeah, I remember that," and I might say, "Well like—I mean my writing wasn't that great then, but what did I think of it then?" and so then I could look back on this and know what happened, and I was also sort of writing it for my teachers, so they'd know what I thought about my work.

Sharon sees two audiences here, her teachers and herself, and two time periods, the present and the future. In writing for her teachers, she has a current goal in mind; she wants them to know what she thinks about her work. When she thinks about herself as the audience, she is thinking about the future and what it will be like to look back at her work over time. Her self-as-audience is a future self.

When I ask her if she thinks of her parents as a possible audience, she is uncertain. This question, however, provokes a lengthy conversation about the ways that she might write differently depending on the nature of her audience. Her astute reading of the quality of trust in her relationships provides clear guidelines for what she will allow herself to say. This same detection of trust mediates her capacity to maintain connection with her own knowledge. A detailed examination of her thinking about audience provides important insights into the connections between trust in her relationships and trust in her knowledge.

> Well, when I wrote it, I wasn't thinking about writing it for my parents, because I thought—I mean, if my parents want to know what like, I think about my work, they just ask me. . . . They'd say like, "What do you think of the work you're doing on your [Metropolis] project? Like, do you think it's good?" . . . With parents, you'd be more open to say like, "Well, I mean, [I] think it's good, but I hate the project or something." With teachers, you wouldn't tell that to the teachers because they like, chose the project, and so you sort of have to think of a way of putting it that's different that might change the way they interpret it.

This passage reveals her sharp distinction between what she might say to her parents and what she would share with her teachers. While she would be "more open" with her parents, she would withhold more from her teachers. When I ask her why she would not tell her teachers her opinion of the project, she responds:

> I mean, if it was like, the teacher like you or Rosie[1] or something, then I wouldn't, then I'd feel comfortable doing that. But with some teachers, I'm sort of like, I don't know like, I'm afraid, I don't know what they'll say when I say that.

Here she distinguishes between her various relationships with different teachers and what she might say in those differing contexts. I am especially attuned to her comment about fear of telling some teachers what she thinks, and I ask what she is afraid of. She responds, "I like, don't want to offend people, because I know that it's not very nice." I ask whether she thinks her current teachers will be offended by her opinions, and she responds decidedly, "It like depends on how it was put." As if to clarify the whole discussion, she adds, "Some of those things I'd feel free saying to some teachers, and some I wouldn't feel free saying to some teachers." She finishes this story by telling me that she never would be able to tell her real thoughts to her previous teacher, Vicki, who many students described as volatile.

> I don't know, it's like, 'cause my teacher Vicki, who was my teacher before, I wouldn't, I would never have been able to say that to her 'cause she would have got like really mad, and she would have just like, blown up if I said any of those things. And so that's like, who I couldn't say it to.

In this narrative, Sharon thoroughly explores the issue of audience. She begins by explaining that there is a clear difference between talking to her parents and her teachers. She feels that she can be free with her parents in a way that she cannot be with her teachers. As we begin to disentangle the threads of this issue, she also explains that she can speak differently to different teachers. She locates the freedom she perceives with teachers with whom she has long-standing and close relationships, such as Rosie (her other first/second grade teacher) or me.

Whereas previously she described modulating her voice in order to be perceived well by the teachers, in this section, she describes editing her ideas in order to be nice, not to offend, and to protect herself. She may be concerned about how her teachers perceive her, but her focus is on not wanting to insult her teachers.

While Sharon's capacity for empathy is strong here, I wonder how the tenor of her relationships with her teachers and the consequent self-editing shape her capacity to know the thoughts she is not sharing. In thinking about this question, it is useful to listen to her narrative through the "I" voice. In the first section, when talking about her parents as audience, the "I" voice is in dialogue with "they" and "you" and is actively thinking, as revealed by her phrases: "I wrote. . . . I thought. . . . I think. . . . my work. . . . I mean, I think. . . . I hate. . . . " When imagining how she would respond to her teachers, she begins with a more distant, tentative "you" voice: "You wouldn't tell. . . . you sort of have to think. . . . " She returns to an "I" voice that is actively sorting out what she can say and what she should withhold. For teachers with whom she is connected, she says, "I'd feel comfortable." With other teachers, however, the verbs convey a sense of withholding thinking and actions and are fraught with negative emotions: "I'm sort of. . . . I don't know. . . . I'm afraid. . . . I don't know. . . . I say. . . . " The acts of holding back and self-editing are palpable. While she begins talking about teachers in a more distanced "you" position, as if to distance herself from her teachers and herself, she reclaims the "I" voice, even as she struggles to hold on to her knowledge in the face of imagined conflict.

As she imagines the conflict that would ensue from telling her teachers her real opinions, her language becomes more tentative. The "I don't know" phrase creeps into her speech with even more force. Most profoundly, she feels that she loses the capacity to speak:

I wouldn't

I would never have been able to say that

I said

I couldn't say it.

I am struck by this last "I poem," because until this point, Sharon's capacity to know what she knows, even in the face of disagreement, has been bold. Yet in the face of imagined conflict, her knowledge becomes more tenuous. Hand in hand with this phenomenon, her capacity to speak diminishes profoundly. The "be nice, don't offend" culture, with its silencing effect—often described by researchers of adolescent girls as the root of the underground[2]—wields tremendous power over Sharon's capacity to say what she knows. And yet, maintaining her tenacious grasp on her "I" voice, she holds on to her knowledge and is conscious of the loss of her voice.

Two years after the interviews, Sharon read the transcripts, and she took special notice of the varied knowledge she selected to share, depending on her audience. She said that this was "really true" about herself. She was visibly pleased when I told her how important this idea is to my understanding how students learn in school. In the course of a couple of hours, I was fascinated to watch her report this finding four different times to her mother, her father, her brother, and to Rosie, her former teacher at the Terrace School. Clearly this issue was still a live one for her.

Locating Confidence

In thinking about Sharon's understanding of audience and the care she takes to distinguish between what she knows and what she will say, I want to understand how she so skillfully protects her knowledge from dissociation. That is, in suppressing her voice, so as not to offend, to be nice, to make sure teachers get the right idea about her, how does she not lose connection with that protected knowledge? In her discussion of audience, she demonstrates this protection beautifully, even in the face of conflict, when her capacity to speak is most at risk.

Sharon reveals that a key source of her strength and resilience resides in the idea of confidence in herself. Her initial discussion of confidence occurs in the first interview, when I ask her whether she can recall a situation in which she did not know that she knew something. I am curious as to whether Sharon's strong grasp of what she knows changes when she feels that she does not know an idea or concept. This proves to be an easy question for her. She swiftly describes learning the different properties in algebra and her difficulty retaining and understanding the uses of these properties. I ask whether she was bothered by the idea that she did not understand these mathematical concepts. I ask this question because Sharon is a strong mathematician and takes pride in her facility with number concepts. She responded by saying that she was not upset, because she knew she would eventually understand the concept.

> I wasn't upset or anything, because I mean, especially in that case, as we were going ahead. I mean, I wasn't expecting to know, to understand it all, but I mean, I don't really get upset. I mean, even if it takes me a few, like the teachers have to explain it a few times or if they have to give me a piece of paper. I don't really, I mean, I might get frustrated because I still don't understand it, but I don't get upset like, "Oh, why can't I do this?". . .
>
> I mean, it's sort of like I'm confident enough that I know that even if I don't get it now that I mean there's always enough—that even if the teachers explain it . . . and I still didn't understand it, there's always something else I can do to understand it. I can go, I can ask my parents or my brother if they know something.

In this story, Sharon locates one source of her strength in the word "confident." She explains that even if she does not understand, she is confident enough to know that she will eventually understand. Her use of "confidence" here embodies a critical aspect of trusting herself and those around her. She knows that if she does not "get it" now, she can seek out resources to gain understanding. She sees her family as a key source of support.

At the same time that I hear Sharon's trust in herself and her family, I also hear her struggling to keep the confidence in place. When faced with concepts she does not understand, not only does she seek help in understanding, but she also seeks out support to shore up her trust in herself. The phrase "I mean" noticeably creeps into her narrative. The story through the first-person voice sounds like this:

I wasn't upset

I mean

I mean

I wasn't expecting to know

I mean

I don't really get upset

I mean

I don't

I mean

I might get frustrated

I still don't understand

I don't get upset

why can't I do this

I mean

I'm confident

I know

if I don't get it

I mean

I still didn't understand it

I can

I can go

I can ask

The seven times that Sharon says "I mean" in this short story (in contrast to using it ten times throughout the rest of the interview) are signals that she is trying to make sure I understand her and that she is not entirely sure of herself.[3] Sharon's use of "I mean" suggests that, while she is connected to her knowledge, when confronted with situations such as the math story, she feels those connections being undermined. Yet her repeated "I can" phrases at the end of the narrative suggest her sense of her own capacity and agency. She is actively struggling against the forces that urge disconnection. This interchange indicates that while confidence cannot ward off the assaults on her knowledge that can leave her feeling shaky, it can bolster her capacity to resist disconnection from what she knows.

When I ask her to talk about a time when she knew something but did not trust herself, she tells another math story—this time with less struggle. Focusing on what it feels like for Sharon to know without trusting herself, I realize that I am trying to ferret out the difference between confidence and trust. Speaking quickly, in a definitive tone of voice, she recalls:

SHARON: Like this year, again it was like math in the algebra group. We had one really long problem, the order of operations, and it had something like, I forget what it was, but it was in some form that was really confusing, and I was like, "Well, I think I'm supposed to do this," but I was like, really—I was pretty unsure; I was like, but it also could have been this or this.

MIRIAM: So what did you do?

SHARON: Well, at first I tried it my own, my like, way, and I looked at it, and, and I didn't know if it was right; and then Jon was standing there, so he showed me. He like, said, "Okay, well, first you do this, and then . . . " So like, after he showed me the first few steps, I was like, "oh yeah," and then I could do like this.

In this story, Sharon knew that she understood the concepts but was not sure of their application. She knew that she could find the tools to solve the problem but did not believe that she had ready access to those tools. She sought out help from a reliable source, her brother, and solved the problem. As she tells this story, her voice steadies and she is more secure in her knowledge. She says "I mean" twice, but the "I" voice has settled into a bold voice that describes her strategies for learning.

She knows her intellectual steps as revealed by her "I" statements: "I forget. . . . I think. . . . I'm supposed to. . . . I tried. . . . I looked. . . . I could do. . . . " Her ability to reflect on her thinking processes is keen. Though the word "like" persists, she no longer makes sure that I am following her with connections such as "I mean" or "you know." A lack of trust in her knowledge does not seem to shake her confidence in the way that the prior experience of not knowing undercut this sense of self.

Interestingly, in an episode lacking trust in self, she turns to a trusted other to help locate what she knows. She does not employ her internal confidence as the nurturing force in her knowledge; she turns to her brother, a trusted other. In the earlier story, in which she felt she did not know, she turned to her internal trusted self, her confidence, to support her quest to build this important knowledge. In lacking knowledge, she turns to her own confidence. In lacking trust, she turns to a trusted relationship to reclaim the trust.

Just when I think I understand the distinction between trust and confidence, Sharon unearths yet more complexity in this essential aspect of her epistemology. In the second interview, Sharon returns to the concept of confidence and paints a visual picture of what confidence looks like in her daily life at school. The term surfaces when Sharon describes the way she knew that she had improved as a writer:

> I am more confident like about it. I mean, I used to write
> . . . and I might not be that confident that I'd be able to
> like read it to someone and that they would think the
> same thing I thought. But now I feel more confident
> that—I mean, like, I could go out into the hall and like,
> read it to someone and that they wouldn't be like "Oh,
> this writing is so bad."

In this description, Sharon imagines standing in the hallway at the Terrace School, reading her writing to someone walking down the hall, and feeling sure of the quality of her work. She can visualize the growth of her abilities to write and to feel strong about her writing. She has a clear sense of the growth in her writing as well as a stronger trust in her capacities as a writer.

In this "hallway story," I am struck by Sharon's strong "I" voice and her steadfast grasp on her own understanding of her knowledge. This imagined encounter, in which she confronts the possibility that someone might disagree with her assessment of her work, does not seem to erode her trust in what she knows. She does not worry about offending the hallway passerby. This response is markedly different from her imagined conflicts with her teachers, in which her "I" voice became shaky and less secure.

In thinking about the differences in Sharon's reactions to these imagined potential conflicts, I am fascinated by the presence of confidence in this narrative as a force that supports Sharon's trust in herself and buffers her from the internal volatility that can come from conflict, whether it is real or imagined. From this story, I learn that not only can confidence bolster her capacity to know but it can also reinforce her capacity to trust herself.

If confidence plays such a central role in her capacity to know and to trust, I wonder how she nourishes and sustains this key aspect of self. Sharon offers insight into this question as the second interview draws to a close. As she reflects on ways that self-assessment work can help her, she describes how locating her "strongest point" in writing helped her continue with a writing project with which she was having "trouble." As we continue to talk about how she responds to self-assessment questions such as "What are your strengths?" she deepens her explanation of the importance of locating her strengths as a means for shoring up her confidence:

> Instead of having someone say, "Oh yeah, that's like, really good!" It's sort of like—it's sort of like you're

telling that to yourself instead of having to have someone say that to you.

Like Gabe, whom we will meet in Chapter Five, Sharon feels that
telling herself her strengths is more empowering than hearing that
voice externally. She emphatically explains,

> I mean, if it's my project that I'm doing . . . I want to like
> it. I don't want it to be that, like, if everyone else likes it,
> but I hated it? Then I wouldn't want to have it; then I'd
> want to have a different project or something.

Though Sharon does not name "confidence" in this interchange,
she describes the experience of feeling confident about her work. It
would not be enough for others to say that her work was good. She
needs to find the resources to help her see the strengths in her work,
because she wants "to like it." Creating and nourishing a relationship with herself and her work, in which she can sustain an internal dialogue that recognizes her disposition as a learner, is key to
nurturing her confidence. This confidence buffers her against assaults on her knowledge. In other words, it is an engaged relationship with self that sustains her confidence, that sustains her capacity
to remain connected to her knowledge. From this perspective,
Sharon teaches me that "confidence" is a relational construct, reflecting her relationship with self in the context of relationships
with others. For Sharon, confidence protects and sustains her capacity both to trust and to know. Confidence is the connective tissue
between trust and knowledge that helps her locate her words and
say what she knows.

Thinking About Sharon

The conversations with Sharon reframe the way I think about the
ideas of communication, audience, and confidence. I learn to see
these terms as relational cues, as words that alert me to key aspects

of classroom relationships that shape students' capacity to learn and to say what they know. In thinking about communication, Sharon reveals her concerns about being perceived well, not wounding or affronting anyone with her words, and not creating conflict. This kind of self-editing does not appear to affect her capacity to know her thoughts and ideas, but it does intensify her struggle to locate words that represent her thoughts.

It is Sharon's discussion of audience that reveals the centrality of her most reliable relationships in maintaining her trust in her knowledge and resisting the pressure that might cause her to disconnect from her knowledge. She is careful, when dealing with relationships that she views as unreliable, to speak judiciously. Again, she guards thoughts and ideas that might jeopardize how she is viewed, that might be viewed as offensive, or that might cause conflict. Similarly, she takes care to protect the knowledge that is developed within these relationships, looking for supports to buffer the assaults that an unreliable relationship can bring.

Sharon's construct of "confidence" provides fundamental protection and support of her knowledge. Born in the context of trusting relationships and nourished by opportunities to view herself as a learner, this confidence allows her to recognize her capacities as a learner, trust her emerging ideas, and articulate the knowledge she values.

In both listening to Sharon's stories and watching the dynamics of the interview, I feel as if I'm hearing Sharon's ideas in surround-sound. As in other interviews, the relational dynamics of the classroom are often mirrored in the dynamics of the interview. Sharon describes her difficulty in writing her ideas and the phenomenon of the flow that comes after she gets started, and I see this process occur in the interview. Often when we first start talking about how she knows her thinking, she struggles to find her words. When she finds a comfortable point of departure, her ideas flow, and she is able to find her words and her sentences. As I watch Sharon navigate our conversation, shy away from the questions that do not connect for her, and engage the questions that are meaningful to her, I see the finesse she has developed in looking for constructive avenues for saying what she means. I see the tools she searches for and uses in building the confidence to know.

Notes

1. Rosie is Sharon's other first/second grade teacher.

2. Brown & Gilligan, 1992; Gilligan, 1991.

3. In their study of adolescent girls, Brown and Gilligan explain this narrative motif of "I mean" as a girl's "struggle to connect herself with knowing, her mind with relationship" (1992, p. 133).

5

Gabe

Examining Two Kinds of Body Knowledge

A s Gabe and I settle down to our first interview, I am struck by Gabe's physical change over the past few years. He looks big for the chairs in the music room, as if he has outgrown the furniture in the school. He indeed looks ready to graduate. In his sandy blond hair cut short, gentle green eyes, and freckled complexion, I can still see the small boy that I taught when he was seven. At the same time, his angular chin, deepening voice, and tall, sturdy frame suggest the teenager he is becoming. Wearing navy sweatpants, a well-worn T-shirt, and a baseball cap, Gabe's athletic passion pervades his presence. Throughout the interview, he taps the table, twists a rubber band, and rocks on his chair. Though he does not appear nervous, the tapping becomes more persistent during the questions that are hard for him or for which he does not have an immediate answer. I sense that it is difficult for Gabe to keep his body still and that his body is most comfortable in motion.

Gabe and I speak comfortably. Though I have not had much contact with him since I left the school, we easily chat about the class play, graduation, and his next school. I am challenged by interviewing Gabe, because so much of the knowledge that Gabe calls up is embedded in his body. Most of his examples focus on the knowledge he has developed as an athlete, and the issue of trust is deeply connected to trusting his body to perform. As a woman who never found a comfortable athletic identity in my girlhood, I am aware that I cannot easily connect with the feelings or experiences he describes. I see myself pushing for examples of academic knowledge and his subsequent lack of responsiveness. I am also aware in the second interview that I have difficulty in framing follow-up questions because I have not fully understood the depth of his thinking in the first interview. When I reflect on this interview and begin to step into Gabe's shoes as fully as I can, I begin to see his sports stories as breathtaking examples of body knowledge and the complexity involved in learning to trust this kind of knowing. I also see the complexity that teachers face when their students' prevailing ways of knowing differ from their own.

On Listening to Himself

Gabe begins the first interview by staking a clear position that self-assessment is helpful to him because it is a venue where he must listen to himself say what he needs to work on in school. He finds this process much more effective than having a teacher tell him the same information. I find myself thinking about José and the vast difference in these boys' stances.

GABE: I think if the teacher tells you you have to work on a type of math, it doesn't really sink in, but if you look at it and think about it and go, "Well I'm not doing that good in reading or something, I'm not doing good in reading; I have to work on it." It'll tell you more than the teacher just goin', "Well, you're not doin' too good in reading so you should work on it more." [rocking on the chair] So it sinks in more than having the teacher just tell you.

MIRIAM: Why is that true?

GABE: Because you're telling yourself, and when a teacher tells you, sometimes you like aren't listening or don't really care or something.

MIRIAM: So something about you saying it to yourself—

GABE: It's like you're *telling* yourself that. When the teacher tells you, it's like, "Well, okay. So what does that mean?"

Gabe communicates a strong adolescent message of easily dismissing adult opinions, especially those that he views as critical. However, he has a hard time dismissing his own opinions of himself and takes his self-critique quite seriously. Self-assessment affords him an opportunity to dismiss adult opinion, render his own, and have this process of listening to himself invited and honored.

In this short narrative, Gabe uses four different voices to tell the story. There is "I," "you," "teacher," and "it." Listening to Gabe's stance through the cacophony of voices that he has invited into his narrative, I can see the complex dance that is involved in his self-scrutiny.

I	You	Teacher	It
I think			
		the teacher tells you	
	you have to work		
			it doesn't really sink in
	you look at it and think about it		
I'm not doing that good			
I'm not doing good			
I have to work			
			It'll tell you
		the teacher just goin'	
	"you're not doin' too good"		
	"you should work on it more"		
			it sinks in
		the teacher just tell you	

I	You	Teacher	It
	you're telling yourself		
		teacher tells you	
	you like aren't listening		
	don't really care		
	you're *telling* yourself that		
		the teacher tells you	

While he begins this narrative in the "I" voice, saying "I think," the "you" voice soon narrates the experience, in dialogue with the voice of the teacher: "you look at it," "the teacher tells you." The "you" voice holds the place of the self-narrator, switching to "I" when relating to his internal dialogue. The teacher's voice renders an "it"—a critique—that does not sink in, to which the "I" does not listen. When "you," a second voice of self, is in direct dialogue with "I," then the "it" sinks in more. When the teacher dialogues with "you," "it doesn't really sink in." While Gabe is insistent that his self-critique is most effective, he uses all of these voices to tell this story. The rejection of external voices is an integral part of his thinking.

Gabe has such sureness about his perspective on himself that I am curious about how he relates to his sense of knowing. I ask him whether he can think of a time when he knew that he knew something. He easily recounts an extended story of needing to lose weight in order to make the football team. He describes his change in diet and his extreme efforts that included running two and a half hours a day, enveloped in many layers of clothing. He ends this story by describing what he knew about himself:

> I knew I lost it 'cause, one reason it said 120 pounds on
> the scale, and then like the other thing was that I just

felt good. It felt like, good 'cause I lost the weight and
. . . it was really hard, and challenging, and I did it. Now
I know I can do it.

In this story, Gabe describes an internal kind of knowing on a number of levels. He knows how weight feels on his body, so when he
stepped on the scale, he had a sense that he had lost the thirteen
pounds. He also knows that he can work hard and that if he aims
toward a challenging goal, he can meet it. Gabe conveys a sense of
confidence in this knowing. In contrast to the variety of voices he
engaged in describing his knowing in self-assessment work, here his
entire story is rooted in the first-person "I" voice. This knowledge
is firmly entrenched. Listening to this excerpt of his weight-loss
story in the "I" voice, we can hear an unwavering "I."

I knew

I lost

I just felt good

I lost

I did it

I know

I can

The voice of knowing ("I know," "I knew") and the voice of feeling competent ("I can," "I did it") ring clearly in this story. In the
first story, Gabe includes other voices, and while he may dismiss
them, their very inclusion indicates an interactive process of
coming to know. Here, Gabe is describing a knowledge that he
holds deep inside himself. He did not need other voices to con-
firm his knowledge. He knew that he knew the weight and shape
of his body.

Two Kinds of Thinking: "Deep Inside" and "Top-of-the-Head"

Indeed, the notion of "deep inside" knowing is a term that Gabe coins in the interviews. He develops this idea in contrast to "top-of-the-head" knowing. He draws this distinction early in the first interview, and it becomes a reference point throughout both conversations. The fact that these terms are embodied is not an accident. Gabe's stories suggest that he experiences knowledge via his body. As he and I explore these kinds of knowing, I see the depth of Gabe's thinking about how he has come to know what he knows. Gabe's description of what he knows offers a perspective on the varieties of knowledge that children learn to trust in school. His thinking raises questions about the kinds of school experiences that can help students like Gabe develop trust in their wide array of knowledge.

Gabe first uses the term "deep inside" to describe his feelings about school and his ambivalence about going to school.

GABE: I barely miss any school days in the year, and I wish that was not true, but I know like, deep inside me if I did that, if I missed a lot, then I won't get a good education, and I won't do good in anything.

MIRIAM: And it's important to you to do good?

GABE: Deep inside, I guess. I don't really think of it that much at all, though.

I am struck by Gabe's knowledge that he wants to "do good" and that his success depends on a good education. He had commented earlier that he would much prefer to sleep late rather than go to school. While his adolescent body may balk at waking up in time for school, his body also knows that his efforts will help him achieve the goals that are important to him.

The term "deep inside" next appears when Gabe describes an episode in which he did not know that he knew something. He describes playing baseball and struggling to get a hit. He had been a good hitter who "crushed" the ball every time he was at bat. Now he was struggling just to make "good contact." I ask whether he began to doubt that he could hit.

> Umm, sort of in my mind it did. But still deep inside I knew I could. . . . Every time I, every time I made good contact, I'd crush the ball. . . . And I made good contact in a lot of practices, and I sort of knew it was just a matter of time till I crushed a ball and it happened in play-offs. But it was just right before the playoffs. I was struggling, and I wasn't making good contact. . . .

In listening to Gabe's story, I pay close attention to his response to my question about whether his difficulty in hitting pushed him to doubt his capacity as a batter: "In my mind it did. But still deep inside I knew I could." This statement is the first occasion when Gabe differentiates between what he knows in his mind and what he knows deep inside. His batting was not what he expected it would be; it did not match his previous performance, and this shook his trust in what he knew about himself. Yet he did not perceive the knowledge itself to be at risk. This knowing is protected. Deep inside, he believes in his capacity to make contact with the ball. This knowing sustains him through the rough spots of losing faith in his abilities. Interestingly, his "mind knowing" and his "inside knowing" are both situated in the "I" voice, suggesting that both ways of knowing are an integral part of who he is. He is in relationship with both kinds of knowing.

When I ask Gabe to tell me more about deep inside knowing, he offers a second view of this thinking. Rather than describing it as a part of himself or as a way of knowing that is embedded within himself, he describes it as an act in which he stops to consider the ideas in his mind. In this more metacognitive description, he is aware of the processes he engages while thinking. He describes deep inside thinking in metaphorical terms:

> But if you, like, talk, let's say, on-line . . . you have to actually just type it on the keyboard, then it's like . . . a lot better because it's like, you have to—you think of what to say, [*yawns*] then it goes through your mind, and it has to go down to your fingers when you type it. And then you look over it right before you send.

In using this e-mail metaphor, he explains that deep inside thinking is a multistep process: considering what he is going to say; the act of saying it, which is a physical process (it goes down to his fingers); and reflecting on what he has said. Interestingly, I notice that this description of deep inside thinking is situated in the "you" voice. I wonder whether this narrative position indicates that he feels less sure of or less connected to this view of deep inside thinking.

When I ask him to describe the other kind of thinking, what I had heard as his "mind thinking," I refer to it as something he might say off the top of his head. He picks up this label and uses it liberally to describe the kind of thinking that is not deep inside.

> I'm like, the top-of-my-head time. That point. [*I try to say something, but he keeps going.*] It's like in baseball, it's, there's a play, and you have instinct, and you turn around, and nobody's yelling what bases to run to, and you know the . . . the base runners, I mean, are running, and you don't know where they are. You just turn around, and the little instinct and it's, it's, like, mind.

I reflect back that "instinct" sounds like an apt way to describe this "mind thinking." Gabe responds and brings back the top-of-the-head terminology:

The top-of-your-head probably [is] just right off. Quick, not deep inside. 'Cause if you hold the ball and you hold the ball and you hold the ball and actually think about it, and the [player] is going to be rounding third and going home.

The knowing that Gabe describes here is situated in his mind and is quick. This knowing is not considered or reflective, because it is the kind of knowing that has to be used almost reflexively; otherwise, the base runner will be rounding third base before the player figures out where to throw the ball. Gabe uses the word "instinct" to describe this act that is so much a part of him that he does not have to think about this knowledge in order to implement it. While top-of-the-head knowing is in the mind and quick, there is also a quality of depth or embeddedness to it.

When we begin to discuss the differences between deep inside thinking and top-of-the-head thinking, I am aware that I am looking for distinctions or dichotomies. Gabe resists this kind of categorization. I ask him what kind of thinking he was using in our conversations. He tells me that he uses both:

GABE: Because some of the questions are deep, but some of 'em are like—they're like—what I'm saying is just like top-of-the-head.

MIRIAM: What kind of things are top-of-the-head and what kind of things are deep?

GABE: I don't really know. Umm. . . .

MIRIAM: That's a hard question.

GABE: Probably stuff I really have to think about is the deep stuff, which is like . . . like for the first question you asked. I knew that what you, I knew that what the, like, what we were gonna do today, so I sort of had an idea what I was gonna say. Then you asked, "What have you been good at? What's the blah blah blah?"—like stuff like that. I needed to think about that.

MIRIAM: The questions that you didn't expect, the ones you hadn't—

GABE: [*interrupts*] The questions that I didn't know were gonna come, like I only really knew one of the questions, so that it was gonna be grouped apart and smaller ones, and that's really all I knew. So I had an idea for those, but then like, the ones you didn't exactly know something or you knew you knew something I had to think about, and those were pretty deep.

As Gabe describes the kind of thinking and knowing that he uses in the interview, he recognizes using both kinds of thinking. His "I don't know" statement suggests that he is wrestling with my question, my framing of these two types of thinking as separate entities. He describes how his relationship to the question determines the kind of knowing that he calls up. Questions that he has thought about and has answers readily available require a top-of-the-head response. Questions that he feels he had to think about "were pretty deep."

In the second interview, I ask Gabe more about the two kinds of knowing in relation to his self-assessment work. I am interested in understanding the ways that his embodied knowledge supports his capacities in school. I frame these questions by asking which kind of thinking he used in the Metropolis self-assessment. Again, this frame reflected my efforts to distinguish between the two ways of knowing that we had talked about.

As I try to apply the two kinds of thinking to his school world and self-assessment, Gabe's engagement with the interview diminishes. He fiddles more with the rubber band, almost breaks a fragile footstool, and sounds bored. His energy and vitality return when he brings the conversation back to baseball and situates these ways of knowing in his body.

It is clear that I am trying to understand his ideas in the context with which I am most comfortable—the school context. Gabe resists transferring his schema to this context. I marvel at his resistance to my pressure and appreciate the integrity of his embodied knowledge. He explains:

GABE: Well, it's like everything is a tiny bit deep thinking, because your body, like in sports, if you're good in basketball, it's instinct to dribble and that's from deep inside. . . .

[*sounding animated*] Umm, so it's like you think about it; you don't realize you do, but you're thinking about it. It's like in baseball, you're at shortstop, man on first and second, and there's a pop-up. 'Kay, you're like, before the pitch you should think, 'kay, if it's a pop-up, what should I do? If it's a grounder to first, what should I do; second, what should I do; me, what should I do; third, what should I do; hit to the outfield, what should I do; hit to the outfield behind them, what should I do? Stuff like that. Home run, just let the guy run around the bases, nothing you can do.

MIRIAM: So that's the deep thinking? Right?

GABE: It's sort of like instinct and deep, because you already think about it. You don't realize you are, but you are. If you're a good baseball player and you know the game, you are thinking about it. You don't realize it, but you are.

In this description, Gabe has a clear understanding that reveals the continuum between these kinds of thinking. Resisting my efforts to separate and distinguish the two ways of knowing, he uses the word "instinct" deliberately to describe both deep inside knowing and top-of-the-head knowing. His thinking here reinforces the notion that top-of-the-head thinking comes from a place deep inside. When he acts on instinct, it is top-of-the-head knowing; he does not think about it consciously because it is so embedded within him. In the baseball example, the shortstop considers his possibilities before the pitch comes, and that is deep thinking. When it comes to acting after the pitch, the knowledge is top-of-the-head. Yet this knowing is solidly rooted in the depths of inside thinking.

Gabe helps me understand the subtle and important distinctions between top-of-the-head and deep inside thinking at the end of the second interview. I ask Gabe whether the Metropolis self-assessment changed the way he thought about his work. Given his resistance to thinking about self-assessment using the two kinds of knowing model, I am surprised by his response:

> In a way. Not really the top-of-the-head but sort of like how it meant to me. How I wanted it to look. I wanted it to be good; I wanted it to be one of the best work. It's my last work at the school, at the [Terrace] School, and I wanted it to be one of my best. Before that, I didn't really think about it like that.

Gabe introduces an essential idea when he contrasts "top-of-the-head" thinking with "how it meant to me." The Metropolis self-assessment inspired him to consider the meaning of the project. Through this medium, in which he feels that he can be real with himself, he discovers that he wants this last work at the Terrace School to be his best work. He allows himself to uncover his connection to his work in school. The process of finding the meaning of his work is indeed considered and deep thinking. His intention and connection to this idea is evident in the strong "I" voice he uses to tell this story:

it meant to me

I wanted

I wanted

I wanted

my last work

I wanted

Before that, I didn't really think about it.

Not only is Gabe's voice situated in the first person, but he is also clear in his *desire* to find meaning, as is evidenced by the repeated phrase "I wanted." If there is a distinction between these two kinds of knowing, perhaps the essence is in the search for meaning.

On Finding Meaning

Constructing meaning is indeed a central task for Gabe. At the close of the second interview, I ask him to consider the truth of his self-assessment responses. Whereas the other students understood this question as asking them to think about the accuracy of their responses, Gabe used this question as an opportunity to reflect on his accountability to himself. This move is consistent with Gabe's stance that self-assessment is a place to communicate with himself. He begins by saying, "If you're true to yourself, then it'll be true on [the self-assessment]." When I ask him to explain what he means by being "true to yourself," he expands on this idea:

> If you're true, if you tell yourself, if you tell yourself that you're, if you're like, umm, I don't know how to explain this. . . . I know what it is in my head. I just don't know how to explain it. Umm, . . . if you don't cheat yourself, then the answers on this will be correct. . . . If you cheat yourself and say you're better than you are or better than you think you are, say, "Oh, I'm really good at math," and you're just starting to work on it, you say, "Oh, I don't have to work on anything." If you had to work on this part, you're cheating yourself out of it. You're not being true to yourself.

This is clearly a difficult set of questions for Gabe. It is one of the few times in both interviews when he began his thinking with "I don't know how to explain this." He sees the notion of truth in self-assessment work as integrally linked to being true or honest with himself. When he considers what it would mean to portray himself as more able than he actually is, he experiences this idea as "cheating" or a betrayal of himself. In this narrative, he does not mention an other or a "they" who will be judging the veracity of his statements. He stands squarely in judgment of himself. The prominent voices in this narrative are "I" and "you":

I	*You*
	you're true
	you tell yourself
	you tell yourself
	you're
	you're like
I don't know	
I know	
I just don't know	
	you don't cheat yourself
	you cheat
	you're better
	you are
	you think you are
I'm really good	
	you're just starting
	you say
I don't have to work	
	you had to work
	you're cheating
	you're not being true
	yourself

Viewing the narrative through this lens, it is possible to discern an "I" voice that has become unsure of what he knows. The "you" voice is authoritative in asserting the moral lesson of being true to yourself, and the "I" is quiet. As Gabe reflects on his accountability to himself, he enters a stance in which he is unsure. Perhaps the notion of not being true to himself undermines his capacity to articulate or know what he knows about himself. I connect Gabe's idea of being true to himself with the notion that self-assessment can be helpful when he discovers aspects of himself on his own. This self-discovery is a moment when he is honest with himself about how he is doing in school. It is a powerful act that has a significant impact on him. When he entertains the possibility of cheating himself—being less honest with himself—he knows he will lose the capacity to make the self-discoveries. In the process, the "I" voice loses its words and knowledge. When Gabe thinks deeply inside himself and discovers knowledge that is meaningful and feels true, he holds the most powerful sense of knowing.

Thinking About Gabe

Gabe's reflections on self-assessment lead him to talk about the varied ways in which he knows the world. He constructs "deep inside" knowledge that is considered, measured, and time-consuming. It is a process that helps him discover the connections to his work and construct the meaning he derives from his creations and actions. In essence, deep inside thinking is a way for Gabe to build his relationships with his own knowing. When he feels he is not being honest with himself, his knowledge is compromised. When he confronts himself truthfully, he discovers the meaning in his work and locates his capacity to "do good" in his life.

"Top-of-the-head" thinking is no less important. It is the mainstay of Gabe's athletic prowess. One way of understanding top-of-the-head knowing is as a measure of his trust in deep inside knowing. As I heard Gabe explain, top-of-the-head knowing is rooted in prior experiences of deep inside knowing. Once that knowing is secure, he can use it in athletics or even in his interview. Top-of-the-head knowing is not a process Gabe has time to consider. To perform as an athlete, he needs this knowing to be robust and trustworthy so that he can act quickly and decisively. When he loses his confidence in this knowing—for example, when he had trouble hitting—he reaches back into the deep inside knowing to help reestablish the stability of his top-of-the-head knowledge of batting.

Talking with Gabe and reflecting on our conversations raise significant questions for me about the teacher-student relationship. Viewing the interview as a relational situation that parallels teacher-student dynamics in the classroom, I think about the differences between Gabe and me in how we embody knowledge. Gabe's stories suggest that he lives his knowledge through his body. His moments of trust and distrust of what he knows are most acutely experienced in his athletic life. I am less familiar with this way of knowing, and it is not often at the "top of my head." This is not to say that Gabe does not experience such moments of trust and distrust in his academic, emotional, or social lives. However, the public self that he chose to bring to this interview is the athlete, for whom knowledge is enacted in physical performance. Indeed, when Gabe read the interview when he was fourteen, he noticed how much he talked about sports. He smiled and said that he still does that when people ask him about school.

I watch my efforts to dichotomize Gabe's thinking and to bring it back to realms that are more comfortable territory for me. I then watch Gabe's subsequent loss of interest or energy for the question at hand or for the interview. I wonder how this dynamic plays out in the classroom when children bring modalities of knowing or ways of embodying knowledge that are divergent from their teacher's ways of embodying knowledge. To what extent do teachers push or urge students to communicate their knowledge in ways that teachers can hear but that are not organic for the children? What are the consequences of this communicative guiding? Scholars such as Lisa Delpit have found that when teachers have difficulty hearing the wealth of students' knowledge that is outside their own cultural experience, teachers often may silence students' capacity to say and know what they know.[1] My interaction with Gabe suggests that teachers' ways of embodying knowledge can make it difficult for them to hear divergent modes of knowing and can silence students who differ significantly in this respect. This dynamic is similar to the notion of "goodness of fit" between parents and infants. When parents' temperaments differ significantly from that of their infants, the "fit" can be jagged and parents may have difficulty meeting their children's needs or understanding behaviors that are unlike their own.[2]

I view Gabe's exquisite description of his embodied knowledge as an invitation for teachers to broaden our conceptions of knowing. Despite our best intentions, the world of school can often narrow our view of knowledge to academic knowledge. Hearkening to the seminal work of Howard Gardner regarding multiple ways of knowing or multiple intelligences, Gabe's story reminds us that students' deep knowing often lies outside of the classroom.[3]

My interview with Gabe posed the challenge of how we can make space for his type of knowledge in the classroom. He alerted me to the necessity of making such space, not just to be a nice or an "in tune" teacher but because his embodied way of knowing is a way in which he makes meaning of the world, a way in which he constructs his understandings. When I could not make space for these understandings in the interview, his energy and vitality drained away, a look I have seen dozens of times in students. He became fidgety and distracted, a complaint we commonly hear about children, especially boys. When the conversation allowed him to bring his way of knowing to the fore, his energy returned, together with his focus.

In thinking about my conversations with Gabe, I am left with many more questions. As classroom teachers, how do we create open enough communication with our students to hear how they are thinking, instead of trying to incorporate their thinking into our own constructs of knowledge? How do teachers develop the capacity to hear divergent voices and modes of knowing? How do teachers install safeguards against silencing voices that sound unlike our own? These are fundamental questions of teaching and learning that I will return to in Chapter Eight.

Notes

1. Delpit, 1995.

2. Lerner, 1983; Thomas & Chess, 1977. Many thanks to Chaya Roth for offering me these sources.

3. Gardner, 1983.

Part III

The Relational Context of Learning and Teaching

6

Who Is Speaking?
Deciding Which Truth to Tell

*There's a difference between saying what someone
expects just because you know that they expect it and
lying, as in . . . not telling the truth when you know
the truth.*

Abby, age 12

I n the previous chapters, we have heard the detail and nuance of
four children's stories of trust, relationship, and knowledge. They
have given us a close-up, "zoomed-in" view of the ways that their
relationships with self and others, particularly teachers, shape how
they trust what they know. In the next two chapters, we will step
back to get a larger landscape or panoramic view of the relational
context of classroom life.

The biggest surprise in my discussions with the children in this
study was their repeated return to the ideas of "telling the truth"
and "lying." Students as young as six introduced this idea (in pilot
studies), and both girls and boys injected this idea into their narratives.[1] As a teacher of young children, I had not considered the idea
that children might be lying or not telling the truth in their schoolwork. When I began to listen carefully to the ways that they spoke
about telling the truth, I realized that this term held a deep-seated
relational tension, one deserving of careful attention. Just as José's
term "help" was a code word for relationship, "telling the truth"
was an indicator of relational struggle. Examining the relational

dilemmas that students confront when asked to reveal a truth about themselves became of central importance. The facets of meaning embodied in the notion of "truth" help illuminate the essential meeting place of students' relationships with their knowledge and students' relationships with their teachers.

It is not an accident that this issue surfaced in the context of discussions about self-assessment work. Self-assessments ask students to consider and disclose their perspectives on their own learning and work. Self-assessment is a practice in which students must reflect on what they know to be true about themselves and decide how much of that truth to reveal. In talking with the students in this study, it is clear that the self-assessment decision of disclosure is only one of many that they confront during the school day. For example, in a book report, what opinion does a student disclose if she knows her teacher loves the book she is reading? If a student is placed in a lower tracked reading group and understands this to be his teacher's assessment of his literacy abilities, how much knowledge of literacy and books will he share? If a teacher refers only to heterosexual couples as examples of parents, how much will a child of lesbian parents disclose about her knowledge of family life? As the students described, there are many opportunities during the school day for them to assess the kinds of knowledge they can disclose and to decide which truths to tell about themselves.

The notion of multiple truths was a critical lesson that the students taught me. The students articulately described holding multiple truths about themselves and the dilemmas they confronted when juggling these truths, detecting the receptiveness and openness of those around them, and choosing which truths to share and which to protect.

In examining the ways that the students talked about truth, two strands appear. The first concerns what some students called "being true to self." This strand focuses on the effort to adequately represent what they know about themselves. The tensions that students confront involve their relationship to self and their capacity to represent in words what they know to be true about themselves. The second strand focuses on disclosure and the selection of truths that will be honored and received by those around them. In this type of dilemma, students describe telling partial truths or choosing which truth to tell. The tension that students confront here focuses on their relationships with others, particularly their teachers. In examining both strands, it is possible to see the relational complexity inherent in "telling the truth."

Being True to Self

Early in my research, Jon raised the issue of telling the truth without a prompt from me. He explained that telling the truth was directly linked to trusting his knowledge. I return to Jon's words from the Introduction because of his astute capacity to bring together the notions of truth and trust.

> If the kids trust what they know, they can say, . . . "Oh, I know math. . . . I can do long division. I can do decimals. I can *use* decimals." But if they don't know what they know, [they say,] "Ooh, I'm not so sure about long division." . . . They write things that really aren't true, but they just don't know it about themselves yet.

For Jon, if he can trust what he knows, then he can talk about himself in ways that feel true. If, however, he begins to doubt his knowledge, he might end up writing things about himself that are untrue—for example, that he doesn't know how to do long division. Jon describes a strong link between trusting his knowledge and having a genuine picture of himself that he can share with his teachers. The issue of telling the truth is primarily a reflection of Jon's relationship with his own process of knowing.

Gabe also describes telling the truth in self-assessment as an internal dialogue about his knowledge. Gabe considers telling the truth to be a measure of his personal accountability as evidenced by his concern for being true to himself. As with Jon, the prospect of not being true to himself raises the risk of losing his capacity for knowing what he knows or losing the ability to trust his knowledge. Seeing his potential for being dishonest with himself, he worries that he will lose the capacity to make discoveries and find knowledge that is meaningful.

Daria, age twelve, also views telling the truth as an internal conversation. Daria's worry about being truthful makes self-reflective tasks particularly onerous for her:

> I wanted to make [the self-assessments] be . . . true. I was worried about making them be true, so maybe that's why it was hard. . . . It was something that I wanted to get over with, but I also wanted them to be true and thoughtful. . . .
>
> It's hard to write what's really true for you . . . because sometimes I just don't know. I just can't. If I think about it sometimes . . . I just start . . . thinking about other things instead of that because I just want to escape.

Daria articulates the complexity of deciding what constitutes a "true" answer. Indeed, sometimes she really does not know if her comments are accurate reflections of herself, and the weightiness of this dilemma makes her want to "escape." She worries that her writing may not represent her internal truths.

> I always . . . think I hope that what I've said is true, . . . because I don't want to give you all this information and then I think, "Oh I'm just saying that because I need to say something."

Daria worries that her desire to complete her schoolwork clouds her ability to write an accurate representation of her thinking. The stakes of her struggle are high because she knows that she is sharing her ideas so that her teachers can know her perspectives on her learning. While she is concerned about being honest with herself, she also wants her teachers' knowledge of her to be accurate.

For Jon, Gabe, and Daria, the issue of truth reflects an internal dilemma of trusting their knowledge so that they can perform well, make meaning of their work, and articulate a realistic reflection of what they know. As Daria suggests, this process can be so difficult that the student wants to escape from its weightiness. Yet all three students' words indicate that trusting what they know is a key aspect of being able to locate their internal truths. Their words and stories reveal the tensions of constructing this internal trust, which leads to experiences of "truth."

Telling the Truth, But Not All of It

In contrast, Emily and Becky offer perspectives on "truth" that focus primarily on the tensions of trust in their relationships with their teachers and peers. Emily, age twelve, sees gradations of truth in her work, and while she is fully aware of her own opinions and beliefs, she carefully selects the content that she will disclose to her teachers. The criteria for this disclosure are clear. She will only share information that she believes her audience can hear and that will not lead to public embarrassment. Emily has well-thought-out notions about telling the truth. She can describe the gradations and nuances of telling the truth:

EMILY: If the truth . . . is something I really won't write, then instead of just not telling the truth, like lying, then I just don't say it, unless it's totally necessary.

MIRIAM: What do you mean?

EMILY: Well it's kind of like there's a difference between, . . . it might sound irrelevant, but it's not really. Being mean or not being kind, or lying and just not telling the truth.

MIRIAM: Explain that to me.

EMILY: If somebody asks you a question, you might just not answer and that would be not telling the truth. But if you said—if you said something that wasn't true, that would probably be a lie.

Emily distinguishes between not telling the truth and actively distorting the truth. If she feels that she cannot tell the truth, then she silences herself rather than create a fiction to disclose. Just as she distinguishes between "being mean and not being kind," she draws a fine line between "not telling the truth" and telling a "lie."

When I try to understand the difference between not telling the truth and lying, I use the term "avoiding the truth." Emily is sensitive to the nuance of language and takes issue with this term. In explaining her objection to this word, she makes a central point:

MIRIAM: How does it work when you avoid the truth?

EMILY: I wouldn't exactly call it avoiding, but I admit it to myself, and I'd rather not admit it to other people.

MIRIAM: So it's really . . . that you're presenting one thing to the outside world and one thing to yourself, but you know deep inside what is true?

EMILY: Or like I'm presenting the whole thing to myself and only half of it to the outside world.

Emily wants to be clear that though she might selectively tell the truth to the outside world, she does not avoid confronting the whole truth inside herself. This is an essential distinction because in saying this, Emily suggests that she stays closely connected with both the knowledge that she holds inside *and* the knowledge that she shares. One way of knowing does not suppress the other. This idea is highly sophisticated; it indicates her capacity to hold onto multiple truths or multiple stories: the ones she tells the outside world and the ones she tells herself. While one understanding of psychological development suggests that an individual must relinquish relationship with the other to develop self, Emily portrays a much more nuanced and complex psychology. Her explanation resonates with the findings of contemporary relational psychologists who view self and other as inextricably linked and mutually dependent.[2] That is, the truths she constructs to represent her self are intertwined with the ways she reads her relationships with others. Her continued explanation demonstrates these links. She describes how she might withhold the truth, depending on the reaction she anticipates:

MIRIAM: Can you give me an example of a time when you did that?

EMILY: Ahhmm, [*long pause*] well like, in third grade, me and my friends were having a fight, and they said like, "Are you still mad at me?" and part of me was really mad, and part of me wanted to make up, but I just said, "No, no, I'm not mad." Even though part of me still was. I guess 'cause I just—it's like, "Are you mad at me?" "Yes I'm mad at you, now go away." That's kind of. . . . They'd probably hate me forever. . . . I just would rather be friends and still be a little mad than still not be friends.

MIRIAM: Than lose that friend.

EMILY: Yeah, so I just said, you know, half of the truth.

Emily keeps a firm grasp on her own internal reality of being angry and chooses carefully the story she will share (that she is not angry) based on the consequences she believes she will confront (that if she discloses her anger she will lose the relationship).

Emily's stance is tenacious. She holds on to what she knows and resists disconnecting from that knowledge. Her resistance takes the form of silence or "going underground," but it is not a giving up of her internal truth.[3] Emily's stories highlight the tensions between what she knows and what she feels she cannot say. While this is a force that could lead her to disconnect or dissociate from the knowledge she protects, she resists the pressure.

Becky's thinking about telling the truth echoes many of the themes that Emily raises. She distinguishes between things that are "true" and "perfectly true." Becky, age twelve, tells me that she is worried about being publicly embarrassed in class. When I ask her about how the notion of truth affects her schoolwork, she explains:

BECKY: You either do it so that it's true, it's not gonna really embarrass you. Or you do it . . . so that, so that it's perfectly true and just try not to be around when the teacher reads it. [*chuckle*]

MIRIAM: Now do you, well, let's talk about the first part where you do it, where it's perfectly true but . . .

BECKY: But it's not totally what you could answer. It's more, "Okay, this is true. I could write more. I don't want to embarrass myself in front of the whole class, so I'll just say this, and it's true." I mean, they can't complain. It is true that I think [*clears throat*] I'm good at writing paragraphs. I could say that some of my paragraphs aren't as good as they could be, and I could write that. But I don't want, but the teachers will no doubt talk about it in the room in front of twenty of us, so I'm just gonna write a very short, sweet, true but not totally, answer.

For Becky, telling the truth reveals an accurate aspect of herself but does not give the full depth of her ideas or feelings. This means finding concise and polite words that do not offer many opportunities for exposure. Telling the "perfect truth" means telling everything, and with this, she risks public disclosure. Even though the self-assessment sheets were shared only with the teachers, the truth discussion led to the fear that her responses would be divulged to the larger group. This was a worry expressed by a number of children. Somehow, though the disclosure was in reality only in relationship to her teacher, the ramifications seemed to feel as though the disclosure would be far more public.

Becky echoes Emily's notion of multiple truths. Becky eloquently explains that she might hold one truth about herself, while her teachers' expectations of her may differ. If these "truths" conflict, Becky knows that difficulties lie ahead:

> The teachers, they're always expecting something. Either at the end of the year, it's what they've come to know from experience, and you don't know what they've experienced from you, and you don't know whether it's true or not, but you know they're expecting something. . . .
>
> You know that they've come to know you in some certain way. It may not be true or not, but they're expecting you to answer the self-assessment in one way, and you have no idea of what that way is, but you know they're expecting it.

Becky's ideas here are extraordinary. She astutely labels the profound tension of expectations in teaching and learning relationships. The teachers expect something from her, and those expectations shape the way they see and experience her. I am fascinated by her use of the word "experience" and the idea that teachers have learned from experience with the students, but also that they have *experienced* the student. Often the teachers' experience of the student is information to which students do not have access, but it clearly affects the relationship. Without this information, Becky does not know how to respond to the teachers. Even if she wanted to write what the teachers expected in order to avoid conflict, she could not do so because she does not know their perceptions of her. She is left guessing and worrying about whether her own perspective will be "right" in her teachers' eyes.

BECKY: It's one of the things you think about when you're writing it. Is this the answer they want? Whether it's not one particular answer, question, or kind of question or not. It's one of the things you think about automatically? [*tentatively*]

MIRIAM: Yeah, and what would be so bad if it's not . . . the answer they want?

BECKY: I don't know. It's just one of those things. Am I doing this right? I mean they probably wouldn't do anything. It's just the feeling that you didn't do it right.

Getting it "right" is important to Becky and so practiced that this standard becomes "automatically" present for her when considering her work. The internal pressure of this standard is weighty and serves as a key criterion by which she judges her responses to her teachers.

In fact, the notion of getting it "right" was pervasive in the interviews. Similarly, my prior research with first and second graders also revealed that students wanted to get the "right" answer in their self-assessing work, even though they knew that in reality, there was no correct answer. If they write what the teachers expect, they feel that they "got it right."[4] In this study, "getting it right" is a key cue that suggests that the students are wrestling with the ways their self-perceptions match up with their teachers' perceptions of their work and their learning. Telling the truth is a necessary next step in which they decide how much of their internal reality to share. This decision is heavily dependent on their understandings of their teachers' expectations and experiences of them.

The stories that Emily and Becky tell help portray the interpersonal terrain that the term "truth" encompasses. They articulately describe the criteria they use to select the knowledge they share and the knowledge they suppress. In revealing the tensions of sharing and suppressing, they do not display evidence of dissociation from the suppressed knowledge. They articulate resilient and tenacious voices of trusting their knowledge and an astute reading of the relational dynamics of learning. They resist forces of disconnection through their rejection of acts of "lying." Lying is not only a moral problem but one that provokes judgment. Lying is also an act that pushes students to disconnect from their internal truths. By selectively telling the truth, they are able to hold on to their full spectrum of knowledge. They also hold steadfast to the essential support of trust both in what they know of themselves and in their knowledge of the relational context in which they live and learn.

Thinking About Truth

Listening to the nuanced and varied ways that the students talk about truth, we can see how this complex relational construct reveals a key intersection in which students' relationships with self and with others come together. When describing the moral imperative of truth, students discuss the importance of being "true to themselves" so that they can access what they know about themselves and make meaning of their work. They tell us that trusting what they know is essential to finding their internal truths.

The students also tell us that when they contemplate telling the truth about their learning and their work, they carefully consider which aspects of self they will share. They carefully gauge which truths can be heard by their audience and then share only what they feel will be well received. By and large, they tell us that they do not disconnect from that which they do not share. Rather, they carefully juggle these internal truths, holding on steadfastly to both the overt and covert stories about themselves and their learning.

When I reflect on the many stories of truth that the students tell, Becky's comment about not having access to her teachers' experience of her raises an essential issue of teaching and learning. Becky knows that her teachers form opinions and judgments about her based on the ways that they experience her in the classroom. She also knows that if teachers give her access to the content of their experiences, if they communicate their perceptions and feelings about her, then she can respond and react.

Her comments urge us to ask how teachers can communicate the ways that they experience their students. This communication would create an open dialogue in which misperceptions and disagreements could be aired and, in Tronick and Weinberg's terminology,[5] "repair" could occur. Difference is the "given ground of knowledge"[6] and is the very place that learning begins. As I learned in my interviewing experiences with the students—Maya and Gabe in particular—the places in which their world experiences so diverged from mine were some of the places in which the most important learning occurred. It was when I changed my stance to listen and give them a chance to make connections and associations that followed their own internal ways of knowing that they were able to build new knowledge and find the words to say what they knew.

Becky's story contains a relational imperative for teachers. Students know that teachers form opinions based on the way that teachers experience students in school. Making these experiences visible and audible allows students to enter into a genuine conversation about their knowledge and the relational context in which they learn. The risk involved in teachers' revealing their experiences of children centers on the anticipated response that students will shape their disclosed truths in such a way as to "get it right"—to meet the teachers' expectations. The challenge for teachers is to craft an understanding of children that allows for multiple truths, that allows them to see students as students see themselves, as their parents see them, as their peers see them. In allowing such a wide view of their students, teachers create an open space in which children can bring many truths to the table.

Notes

1. Raider-Roth, 2004.

2. For a full review of psychological theories of self and other, see Spencer, 2000.

3. See Spencer, 2000, on this form of resistance; also Brown & Gilligan, 1992.

4. Raider-Roth, 2004.

5. Tronick & Weinberg, 1997.

6. Debold, Tolman, & Brown, 1996, p. 105.

7

Who Is Listening?

Deciding What Knowledge to Share

*With parents, you'd be more open to say like, "Well,
I mean, [I] think it's good, but I hate the project or
something." . . . You wouldn't tell that to the teachers
because they like, chose the project, and so you sort of
have to think of a way of putting it that's different that
might change the way they interpret it.*

Sharon, age 12

"Audience" Is a Relational Quandary

When teachers ask me how they can begin to access the ways that
their students read the relational worlds in their classrooms, the first
thing I tell them is to examine their students' understandings of the
audience of their schoolwork. This issue above all others holds the
many strands embedded in the relational context of classroom life.
In considering who will read, view, or otherwise observe their work,
students take into account the kinds of knowledge they will share,
the confidence they feel about that knowledge, the veracity of that
knowledge, and the receptivity—the capacity to receive and listen—of those they perceive to be the audience. If we see the tension of "telling the truth" as revealing the juggling phenomenon
that students employ at school, then the "audience" tension can be
seen as manifestation of *how* students juggle the multiple truths
about themselves. In a sense, "telling the truth" reveals the anatomy

of this phenomenon and "audience" reveals the physiology of this process. Within the tension of audience, the students tell us that this juggling act directly implicates their capacity to connect and disconnect with what they know. In this chapter, they first describe how they hold on to what they know about themselves and resist the forces of disconnection. They then go on to tell us that at times, the forces involved in considering their audience are so intense that it causes them to lose hold of or disconnect from what they know. They tell us that it is a complicated struggle of connection and disconnection. The notion of trust, both in themselves and in those around them, looms large in this struggle.

Resisting Disconnection

Discussions with Sharon are especially useful in illustrating how the issue of audience reflects how she holds on to what she knows in the face of both trusting and ambivalent relationships. She articulately explains the kinds of knowledge she would share and withhold, depending on the nature of her readers. As she tells me in Chapter Four, she has one set of responses for her parents, another for her current teachers, and yet another for teachers with whom she feels she has a strong relationship. Listening closely to her stories, I find that she does not compromise what she knows through this selecting process; she knows the knowledge she is suppressing.

The only time her knowledge appears to be at risk is when she holds an opinion that is in conflict with her current teachers. Sharon's ideas about conflict, echoing the findings of Brown and Gilligan,[1] suggest that the costs of conflict, of losing connection with significant figures in her life are so high that at times it is adaptive to let go of what she knows to be true. Yet the cost of letting go of her knowledge of self is also high, for she loses confidence and trust in what she knows, thereby rendering it more fragile. In confronting the issue of conflict with teachers, Sharon's story raises questions of how teachers can create environments in which differences of opinion can be aired safely without provoking judgment, punishment, or loss of trust in what students know. The value of such an environment is most clearly visible when we consider the consequences of this "brilliant but costly solution"[2] or "central relational paradox"[3]—the letting go of relationship to maintain relationship.

Emily employs strategies similar to Sharon's when she describes the different truths she reveals depending on her perceived audience. To illustrate her point, she explains that she still likes to read second-grade books and that this is a fact that she has to conceal from her teachers in a way that is both secretive and truthful. When I ask her who she would be concerned about in regard to the truthfulness of her statements, she describes the different reactions she anticipates from her parents and her teachers:

EMILY: Well, my parents, because they *know* me, kind of. . . . Both my parents have seen me reading second grader books, and like, I enjoy them a lot . . . but it's like . . . [if I say,] "I never read second grader books" . . . my dad and my mom will be like, "Hey, that's not true." And then give me this like really, really long lecture about it. And my teachers, I don't really, I'm not really concerned about the teachers, 'cause they don't know me as well as my parents do.

MIRIAM: So . . . you wouldn't want your parents to find you out about lying?

EMILY: Because they might also like, be disappointed in me because I lied about it.

Emily feels she can withhold this truth from her teachers because they don't know her as well as her parents do. She later explains that she would not tell her teachers about this love for fear of "embarrassing myself." Yet she cannot be dishonest with her teachers because if her parents were to find out, they would be disappointed in her. In negotiating these two concerns—not wanting to be embarrassed and not wanting to disappoint—Emily is thinking carefully, sorting the knowledge she must suppress from the knowledge she can share. The prime consideration is *who* will be listening to what she says. These decisions are akin to a relational obstacle course, requiring a firm grasp on what she knows and her trust in her capacity to read and interpret the dynamics of her relationships.

It is vividly apparent in Emily's and Sharon's stories that the issue of audience figures greatly in the girls' negotiation of multiple truths. For these two girls, this negotiation and selective disclosure does not cause them to disconnect or lose faith in what they know (except in cases of conflict, when knowledge becomes more shaky). In both cases, the girls suggest that they present the full spectrum of their knowledge to themselves and are vigilantly conscious about the knowledge they select to share with the outside world. They trust both their knowledge and their reasons for their selective sharing.

Struggling with Disconnection

Abby, Maya, and Emily illustrate the disconnections that can occur when children attempt to adapt their voices in hopes of satisfying their audience. In particular, these girls highlight how their perception of their audience's expectations and the consequent sense of pressure as well as their respect for and the quality of relationship with this audience shape the ways that they connect with their knowledge. Similarly, when considering themselves as the audience of their work at school, confidence in their knowledge and work becomes key to their capacity to access their knowledge.

Abby is especially articulate in explaining the ways in which her audience's expectations can shape the actual content of her writing. Abby's ideas in this regard echo Becky's sense that her teachers' expectations influence the veracity of her articulated knowledge at school. While Becky makes a clear differentiation between her own ideas and those of her teachers, Abby is perplexed by this difference. Using self-assessment as an example, Abby deliberates the authorship of her ideas:

> I think about that kind of stuff a lot, and it's kind of like, some of the stuff you just, like these questions that you answer so much, just get so worn out that you kind of end up answering like, the same thing every time. Like, "What's hard for you?" "Spelling." "What's hard for you?" "Spelling." And it's like, it's really repetitive, and you know, what if one year, I'm like, "Oh my God, it wasn't that hard for me"? I don't know if I'd be able to know. Because it just gets so repetitive 'cause I answer the same thing for a lot of the questions. You're just like, start to answer the same thing because it's kind of what they expect.

With keen insight, Abby describes the tensions of knowing that teachers form opinions and expectations of her cognitive abilities. I am struck by her comment that she might not be able to know if spelling ceased being hard for her, because this expectation has been repeated often and is now ingrained in her thinking about herself. When interviewing her, I wonder if she truly feels confused about what she knows about herself. She is remarkably articulate and self-assured in her public demeanor, and this stance seems in marked contrast to this moment of confusion. Yet she confirms the confusion by pointing to a question about weaknesses in her sixth-grade end-of-the-year self-assessment:

> *Question 11: What do you think your greatest weakness was this year?*
>
> Spelling?? I don't really know. I just say that because it feels like I always say that. I don't even know if it's true anymore.

In thinking about what she writes in her self-assessment, Abby is conscious that her own view of herself is shaped by her teachers' expectations and by her own repetition of these expectations. When she begins to question whether their perspectives are accurate, she is at a loss for locating her truth. She struggles to separate her own internal knowledge from the expectations of her teachers:

> When you think that someone thinks that it's hard for you, . . . and even if you end up not knowing for sure, you'll still think that it's hard for you because you still think that the other person thinks that it's hard for you. Do you follow me?
>
> For however long you've known it and people know your background so much, that it's just if you, if you, if you say, you know, something like that it's just going to be blown off, you know, the person's shoulders, because they know and because that's kind of what they expect. So there's a difference between saying what someone expects just because you know that they expect it and lying, as in, you know, not telling the truth when you know the truth.

Abby does not perceive herself to be lying when she writes what she believes to be others' expectations of her. The teachers' expectations hold a certain truth, and while she searches to locate her own knowledge of herself, she relies on their opinions. There is a certain sense of comfort, safety, and even protection of her internal truth that comes in relying on teachers' expectations. By using teachers' expectations as her cover, she does not need to disclose what she really thinks about her weaknesses.

Yet teachers' expectations of her performance can also be a force that makes it difficult for Abby to know what she knows about herself. This narrative is another keen example of how students juggle the variety of truths about themselves as they seek to understand their relationships with their own thinking as well as their relationships with their teachers. In this narrative, we can see that while Abby needs the truth that she sees her teachers holding, this truth can also make it harder for her to access the truth she holds herself. The narrative voice of "you" in this passage accentuates the sense of remove and distance from her own knowledge.

Abby's spelling story echoes the sense of pressure that Maya experiences from teachers' expectations. Maya explains that when her teacher viewed her math skills as weak, she too perceived her math skills as inadequate:

> My teachers seemed to think that I was behind in math when I, it was like, I never realized by myself, and they kept pushing it on me, so I was like, "Well I'm not good at math."

In this narrative, Maya realizes that her teachers' perceptions of her abilities shaped her own perceptions. When her teachers viewed her as more competent and placed her in a more difficult math group, her confidence, or in her words, her "self-esteem" grew strong.

Similarly, when Maya feels pressure from her teachers to disclose her weakness, she experiences confusion about the truth of her responses:

> Sometimes when you're doing self-assessments, you feel all this pressure to say what you are not good at. . . .
> And then I'm like, wracking my brain and thinking, well, I have to write something, so I'm going to say that I'm not good at this. When you never know if it's true, and even with the things that I am good at, and you never know if that's true, either.

Maya's comments about truth are directly related to the pressure she senses from teachers to identify feelings about herself that are difficult or stressful. In the face of expectations from her teacher to render an answer and her struggle to locate these experiences, she doubts the truthfulness of her responses. She begins to doubt what she knows about herself.

Abby describes the struggle to hold on to her knowledge in the face of others' perceptions. When talking about her writing, she explains how she moderates her opinion of her work so as to protect herself from harmful critique and to allow herself the thrill of hearing positive feedback.

> I know this is probably bad and it's probably like, not right at all, but sometimes when I hear it from other people, I know that that's like, not really, you know, right, and "the [Terrace] way" or whatever, [*we laugh*] but it's like, you know, I can. Because it's like, the opposite way. If I'm sitting there and I'm like, "This is the best story I've ever written," and like, Tanya comes over and she's like, starts to read it and she's like, "What's this about? I don't quite understand," you know. And then, you know, the teacher comes over and she's like, um, "The comma goes there, ahem, ahem," and then she's, and then she's just sort of marking things on the paper, and she's like saying, "Maybe you should change the plot a little bit," and I'm thinking this is the best content I've ever done. Then you know, it's gonna, you know, pee on my parade, [*we laugh*] but it's like, I'm like, you know, staying, like, on the middle level, and then someone tells me this is like, a really good story? Then I'm like, "Yay." Same as if I'm on the middle level and someone tells me it's not so great, I'll usually wait till someone tells me it is great, so I can get onto the higher level. You know what I mean?

In this remarkable narrative, Abby describes a powerful negotiation in which she knows her opinion of her writing but stays on a "middle level" of conviction or confidence in this knowledge. When her knowledge is disconfirmed by a friend, Tanya, or by a teacher, her lack of confidence shields her from the disappointment that comes with these judgments. When her knowledge is supported by an outsider, then she can move to a "higher level" and trust what she knows about her work. With carefully chosen images, Abby describes the force embedded in the response of her audience that can help her trust or step away from what she knows about her work.

I pay close attention to the beginning of this narrative, in which Abby seems to apologize for this perspective by saying "I know this is probably bad and it's probably like, not right at all." She has a sense that she should have confidence in her work and in her opinion of her work. She admits, sheepishly, that sometimes when she hears feedback or support from other people, it makes a difference in her perception of her work. She acknowledges yet again that this perspective goes against the grain of her school, which advocates for children's ownership of their ideas and work: "I know that that's like, not really, you know, right, and 'the [Terrace] way' or whatever, but it's like, you know, I can." In acknowledging that others' perspectives shape her own, she takes an active stand against the acculturation and expectations of the school. In other words, while she seems to search for public acknowledgment to affirm her ideas about her work, she has little trouble acknowledging her resistance to public (that is, her school's) expectations about how she should attain this affirmation.

Respect Begets Confidence

Abby's stories are particularly helpful in illustrating how the quality of the teacher-student relationship figures into her capacity to access and say what she knows in school. Abby deepens her explanation of how her audience can shape her own perception of her work—how it affects her capacity to move to a "higher level" (or a lower level) in assessing the quality of her work. She points out that her own responses depend in large measure on the quality of her relationship with a given listener. She identifies respect for her audience as a key ingredient in a quality relationship.

> It's easy to jump to the high level, and . . . if someone's like, "I don't quite understand," they're like, "This is not, you know, such a good story," I'm just like, ehhh, and then [*in a very animated voice*] I take it, and I think about it, and then I think. And then if I agree with it—'cause it's always about if *I* agree with it—and if I don't agree with it, then tuppence to them. You know what I mean? And so it's like, I take their feedback, and if I think like, "Eh, they don't know what they're talking about," then it's just like, they don't know what they're talking about. But then if it's like, um . . . [*her voice quiets*] I think that they're a really good writer, and they have really good feedback. . . .
>
> For example, I had like, a tutor . . . who's a writer, and she's like really awesome. . . . She's just great, and she reads all this poetry with me, . . . and she makes me talk about it and makes me write poetry and everything. So when I bring it in, if she said that, you know, this isn't like my best poem, and she has reasonable feedback or even unreasonable, I'm gonna be like, "Okay, I need to work on it harder," because it's someone that I know is a really good writer and who I really respect.

In this narrative, Abby identifies "respect" for her audience as a central factor in how she processes the feedback on her work. If the other is someone she perceives to not "know what they are talking about," she can dismiss their opinions and hold on to her own perspective. In this type of relationship, she asserts her self strongly, as evidenced in her comment "'cause it's always about if *I* agree with it—and if I don't agree with it, then tuppence to them." Yet Abby will wait for someone like her tutor, someone she really respects, to help her jump to a higher level. Taking the step to achieve that higher level of confidence in her work is directly connected to the confidence that a respected other holds for her.

The notion of confidence is central when Abby considers her self as her audience. When she feels confident about her work, then she feels that she knows the concepts or issues with which she is grappling. In certain cases, her confidence supersedes the opinions of those around her. She offers an example about learning about borrowing and carrying in math. If she uses this method to solve the problem, she relates,

> I'm just doing like, what they say, and then I'm checking it, you know, the other way because I don't know why I put the "1" up there and then it comes out to "2," and I don't even know what the "2" means. I don't know if the 2 means 2000 or, you know, 2 tens. . . . And then if the teacher comes over and, you know, I've erased all this stuff on the side of the page, and she sees I have all the answers right, she's like, "Wow, you really do understand this, don't you?" and . . . I would, I don't know what I would say. I would probably say, "Yeah I do." And [*laughs*] I don't, you know, because I just did it the other way I knew or I wasn't confident that I had it right. Probably a good word: if I'm not confident about it, I don't understand it.

In this case, Abby's teachers offer positive feedback that, according to her prior theory, could help her get to that "higher level" of trusting her knowledge. Yet she knows that she was following a rule or an algorithm without understanding the mathematical concepts involved. Without her internal confidence, she does not feel that she really knows what she knows. In a sense, she is describing

Damasio's notion of a "core sense of self" that integrates her experiences. In hearing Abby talk about confidence, I am reminded of Sharon's conviction that confidence is central to trusting what she knows.

Abby's thinking about audience is complex. It demonstrates the nuance and multiple layers of thinking that coincide with thinking about the omnipresent issue of who will read her work. Abby relies on the opinions of others, especially those whom she respects. Yet she does not take in others' perspectives easily, and she considers their knowledge and authority before she decides whether their opinions matter. Nevertheless, she often withholds total conviction about her own work until she can hear the assessments of others. In these cases, her capacity to connect completely with her knowledge is facilitated by the support of a respected audience. Yet, total *understanding* is predicated on her own internal confidence. Abby suggests a fascinating idea about the nuance embedded in the notion of connection to both others and herself. To allow herself to get to a "higher level" or complete investment in her work—one type of connection—she relies on feedback from a respected other. To feel certain that her understanding is strong—another type of connection—she relies on her own internal confidence.

Thinking About Audience: The Connection/Disconnection Dance

When we examine the ways that students talk about the notion of audience, they offer us a close-up view of their understandings of the relational dynamics in school. They clearly explain that the decisions they make regarding withholding and sharing knowledge depend largely on their perceptions of their audience. They consciously make these decisions and can articulate the factors they consider.

First, the students consider the *type* of relationship they have with the audience. They discern the differences between what they might say to a parent, a teacher, a student teacher, a new teacher, a former teacher, or a peer. Second, they examine the *quality* of the relationship. Is their relationship with a given person a trusting, respected, and safe one? Is it a relationship with a long-standing history? How has this person responded in the past? Third, they consider how their own *self* will be presented and how it will be perceived in the context of the relationship. Will the student embarrass herself with the disclosure of certain kinds of knowledge or information? Will the audience be impressed, disappointed, or hurt by the knowledge shared? Closely related to the idea of presentation and perception of self is the fourth factor, the students' reading of their audience's *expectations and perceptions*. What does the audience expect the student to say about his knowledge? What does the audience expect that the student knows? How has the audience experienced the student in the past? Finally, when the students consider themselves as audience, their *confidence* in themselves is the most important factor in accessing and trusting what they know. As Abby so articulately states, if she has confidence in what she knows, then she probably understands.

In considering these five factors, we can see the sophisticated relational knowledge embedded in students' connection/disconnection dance. The students teach us that their assessments are complex and varied and resist dichotomizing—for example, categorizing knowledge as "private" or "public" or as "truth" or "lies." In fact, in negotiating these factors, students move in and out of connection with what they know, in and out of connection with their audience. The beauty and complexity of this recursive dance require a vigilant eye on the dynamics of relationship, students' understanding of self, and the nature of the knowledge they are constructing.

In listening to the students' thinking about audience, it is remarkable and important to recognize the nuance with which they read the functioning of their relationships with teachers and the school culture and how these readings shape their relationship with their knowledge. Their stories at times have the qualities of an obstacle course in which they carefully dodge, climb, and tumble with each challenge that a relationship presents. Sometimes, students seem sure-footed, holding on to their knowledge in the face of challenge, harmony, or disequilibrium in a relationship. At other times—such as in the face of imagined conflict—when they feel a relationship could be imperiled, they release their connections to what they know in order to maintain the relationship. As Abby describes, they can move in and out of connection with their knowledge in a moment, depending on the aspect of relationship they are considering.

The psychological adeptness that Abby, Emily, Maya, and Sharon exhibit echoes the findings of relational research on preadolescent and adolescent girls over the past two decades.[4] Their narratives validate the notion that girls pay close attention to the relational world of self and others in negotiating the knowledge they can trust and the knowledge they can share. What they are revealing anew is that this negotiation shapes not only their relational knowledge but also their academic knowledge and their learning in school.

The relational adroitness observed here is not limited to the girls in this study. Certainly, José's sophisticated acts of connection and disconnection reveal a close reading of his relationships with his teachers and his consequent moves in and out of relationship with himself and his teachers. He articulately describes the ways in which he must stay in relationship with his teachers in order to get the help he needs, which in turn allows him to stay in relationship with himself. At the same time, he describes needing to disconnect with the aspects of self that can make him feel most volatile, so that he can engage with his schoolwork, his teachers, and other aspects of self.

In a different vein, yet similar in the remarkable psychological flexibility demonstrated, Gabe moves back and forth between the knowledge that runs "deep inside" and the knowledge that is shared with the outside world. For him, maintaining the balance and connection with both forms of knowing allows him to be successful in the highly social and competitive world of athletics as well as stay true to himself.

While one might be tempted to dismiss these students as an unusual group of children, recent research in relational psychology echoes the findings in this study that children closely read their relational worlds and monitor their communication and knowledge accordingly. Certainly, the last two decades of research on girls' relational understandings substantiates these findings.[5] Research on the relational worlds of boys adds to our understanding by demonstrating that throughout their developmental trajectory, boys read their relationships with their teachers very closely and modulate their work and play accordingly.[6] Research also suggests that when boys' relational knowledge is unrecognized or unacknowledged, there can be severe consequences for the boys, such as depression, hyperactivity and feelings of dislocation.[7]

When we unearth children's relational understandings—in particular, how they read us as their audience—we will learn what it takes to be in healthy "growth-fostering"[8] relationships with them. The larger and more far-reaching question is how we, as adults and teachers, will use this new knowledge. If we learn that children are watching how we build relationships with them and are modulating their spoken knowledge accordingly, what impact will that have on the way we teach? This is the central question addressed in the next and final chapter of this journey.

Notes

1. Brown & Gilligan, 1992.

2. Gilligan, 1996, p. 244.

3. Miller & Stiver, 1997.

4. See Brown, 1998, 2003; Brown & Gilligan, 1992; Orenstein, 1994; Pipher, 1994; Taylor, Gilligan, & Sullivan, 1995; Tolman, 2002.

5. See note 4.

6. Browne & Fletcher, 1995; Ferguson, 2001; Gilligan, 2003, 2004; Pollack, 1998, 2000; Way & Chu, 2004.

7. Kindlon & Thompson, 1999; Pollack, 1998, 2000.

8. Miller & Stiver, 1997.

The Relational Learner
Why Classroom Relationships Matter

When we gather the stories, questions, ideas, and suggestions of the students in the preceding chapters, a portrait of the relational learner emerges. We see children who are serious about their learning and who identify the ways that their interactions, connections, disconnections, trust, and mistrust shape how they build knowledge in school.

Looking at students through this relational lens lead us to ask fundamental and sometimes unsettling questions: How can we create classrooms in which a culture of safety and truth prevails, allowing students to bring as much of their knowledge and their diverse selves to the table as they can? What do we as teachers do that inadvertently pushes students to a position in which they feel it necessary to suppress aspects of what they know? To what extent do students read all of our assignments and assessment measures relationally; carefully select the knowledge they believe can be heard; and thereby call into question the validity of these measures as accurate representations of what students know? In a sense, this last question challenges our most basic assumptions about schoolwork. We may assume that when we assign a project, administer a test, or require an essay to be written, the product we receive in some way reflects what students know about the topic, concept, or issue. We must consider the possibility that students are offering a product that is as much a reflection of what they think teachers want or can hear as it is a reflection of what students actually know.

In asking these questions, we reconsider the nature of the knowledge that students are willing to share in school. We reexamine how we can create learning relationships that offer students the opportunity to construct and represent knowledge in which their own ideas and those of their teachers and peers coexist, commingle, and co-inform, so that one form of knowing does not silence or compete with the other. This paradigm shift requires that we fundamentally rethink our practices of schooling. Instead of seeing the objective of school as the production of self-sufficient, autonomous learners, this paradigm sees the primary educative objective as participation in learning relationships that foster the construction of robust knowledge. The relational paradigm challenges some of the most widely held beliefs about education. In "I, Thou, and It," David Hawkins theorizes that the educated person is one who no longer needs teachers, who becomes his own teacher.[1] Even Hawkins, who pioneered the most important educational model of the teacher-student relationship, appears to hold separation and individuation as the goal of schooling. In the relational learner paradigm, the goal of development in schooling or learning would be, in Miller and Stiver's words, to "grow into" relationships with teachers, rather than to "grow out of them."[2]

This paradigm also shifts our attention when we think about peer relationships. Learning is not fostered by generating competition, which forces an individual out of relationship, but rather is nurtured through collaborative enterprises that ask students to listen to and build on one another's ideas.[3] This paradigm shifts our attention away from standardization ("How can I get each child to learn the same thing at the same pace?") to personalization[4] ("How can I get to know each child, so that I can understand what will help him or her learn?").

The Relational Learner Paradigm in Practice

If we begin to look through the relational lens, this research suggests four arenas in which the notion of the relational learner can shape school practice. The first centers on helping children locate and develop their authentic voice. The second involves learning to listen to children's voices. The third focuses on creating regular and dependable practices that respond to student ideas, concerns, and work. The fourth concerns the creation of learning environments that support teachers in knowing their students well. As we examine each of these four arenas, we will explore the implications of the relational learner paradigm for classroom life.

Helping Children Locate Their Voice

To provide a learning environment in which children can voice their relational understandings, the classroom context must elicit each student's voice in all his or her individuality. Creating such a context requires curricular approaches that value the diversity of children's thinking and that provide opportunities for children to construct new ideas that may be different from their classmates'. Such approaches seek to leave space for children to connect to their own life experiences and bring this knowledge into the classroom as the basic building blocks on which knowledge can be built.

Vivian Paley, a veteran early-childhood teacher, personifies this aspect of classroom practice. In her many publications, she documents how she helps children tell the stories of their experiences, their dreams, their fears, and their fantasies.[5] She helps them learn to re-present these stories in pictures, in written stories, and, most profoundly, in acted-out dramas.

For Paley, the location of children's voice is an inherently relational process. She writes, "The act of teaching became a daily search for the child's point of view accompanied by the sometimes unwelcome disclosure of my hidden attitudes. The search was what mattered . . . and it provided an open-ended script from which to observe, interpret, and integrate the living drama of the classroom."[6] Paley understands that the child's point of view, or voice, is accompanied by Paley's own voice and that the endeavor to elicit the child's point of view is a mutually evolving drama. In connection with Paley, the children dictate stories that fill their minds. In connection with their peers, the students act out these stories, hoping their classmates will breathe life into a narrative that helps them make meaning of their internal and external worlds. As a community of learners, or, in Paley's words, "actors," she and the children are engaged in a collaborative search for meaning in which each voice can express itself and be heard: "We are, all of us, the actors trying to find the meaning of the scenes in which we find ourselves. The scripts are not yet fully written, so we must listen with curiosity and great care to the main characters who are, of course, the children."[7]

Learning to Listen to Children's Voices

The children in this study echo Paley's mandate to listen to them. They tell us, however, that eliciting their voices is not sufficient. Even dialogue is not sufficient. Careful listening is essential. Without such attunement, students quickly conceal what is not or cannot be heard, and the tension between suppressing and sharing knowledge builds. The real question is whether we have the tools to hear what students have to say. The most urgent message from the students in this study is that we as teachers must develop the capacity to hear our students' "ways of knowing" by listening to the voice, the body, the culture, the ethnicity in which they say what they know.[8] The puzzle to solve is how we listen when students' ways of knowing differ significantly from our own. How do we listen without imposing our voice, our way of thinking? How do we listen without silencing?

Careful listening is not an innate skill for most people, including teachers. Creating teaching practices that ask teachers to assume a listening stance can assist in the development of this skill. Katherine Schultz theorizes a conceptual framework for listening to support teachers' reflection on their practice.[9] She identifies "listening to know particular children; listening for the rhythm and balance of the classroom; listening for the social, cultural, and community con-

texts of students' lives; and listening for silence and acts of silencing."[10] Schultz's conceptual framework helps us see the many different stances that we need to assume as teachers in order to listen
to the multiple voices—of children, context, environment, and
silence—that are expressed in classrooms.

A critical aspect of learning to listen to the knowledge that students share involves developing structured and collaborative methods for both observing children engaged in their work and looking
carefully at the work they create.[11] The discipline of observation is
essential to learning to see students in all their complexity—their
bodies in motion and at rest, in social interactions with adults and
children, in artistic endeavors, in writing a story, in mathematical
problem solving. The necessary complement to observation is the
art of describing what we see. Quoting Raymond Williams, Himley
and Carini suggest, "We learn to see a thing by learning to describe
it."[12] Structured settings in which teachers work together, sharing
observations, describing individual children, and closely studying
children's work, can create opportunities for teachers to see the
breadth and depth of children.[13] By recognizing what we see and
what we overlook, what jumps out at us and what is more subtle,
we learn to see ourselves as observers as well. We learn what we see
well and when our vision tends to be blurred. We learn that observing others and observing ourselves are integrally linked experiences.
Building on the work of Dewey, Carol Rodgers identifies teachers'
capacity to see or observe and describe as essential aspects of reflection that are vital to teachers' capacity to take "intelligent action."[14]

The power of observation and description asserted itself one
afternoon in a faculty study group at the Robert C. Parker School
in upstate New York. One teacher, Zoe, presented a piece of writing to a group of teachers who gathered biweekly to look carefully
at student work. Using a detailed process called the Collaborative
Assessment Conference[15] that was developed at Harvard Project
Zero, the teachers read each sentence closely, trying to describe
what Serena, the twelve-year-old author, was saying. Zoe had

brought us this piece of work because she was struggling to make meaning of the writing. The sentences seemed loosely connected and meandered in ways that did not seem to make sense. At first glance, the short essay seemed almost incoherent. By the end of the hour, however, we all came to realize that rather than constructing an incoherent narrative, Serena was experimenting with stream of consciousness in her narrative voice, and the meaning of the piece emerged in all its beauty and complexity. While Zoe was moved and inspired by this realization, I was most impressed by her comment to me the following day. Following our meeting, she had gone home and reread all her students' essays. She was amazed, she said, that when she started to reread all the papers, she realized that she was looking in a new way, seeing strengths and features that she had not previously seen. By learning to look closely at one piece of writing with the added insight of a group of colleagues, Zoe was able to see all her students' work with a broader, more open view.

This kind of thinking about teaching and learning—this way of listening and seeing—requires a collaborative effort on the part of beginning and experienced teachers alike. We cannot see our blind spots without our colleagues' gentle and persistent feedback. We cannot see the complexity of children without viewing their worlds from multiple perspectives. Borrowing terminology from the world of relational research, an "interpretive community" is essential to the work of learning to listen.[16] In such a community, observations are shared, multiple perspectives are offered, interpretations are crafted, and both resonances and dissonances are surfaced.[17] Most essentially, questions are constructed, helping teachers analyze their observations and take action.[18] It is the formation of such questions that can be the most difficult.

The children in this study teach us that the "right" questions are the questions that are genuinely our own, as opposed to the questions that we think we "should" be asking. The "right" questions capture our need as teachers to understand our students; they are questions that we think capture students' desire to understand themselves. To find these questions, we have to know our students—their passions, their struggles, their curiosities, their stories. This knowledge is essential in framing questions that will help students think about themselves as thinkers and knowers. The hardest part of this process is knowing ourselves as teachers. This requires keeping a close eye on what we can see, what we shut out, and what our responses sound like to our students. We need to know what we are urgently trying to understand about ourselves and our students. Finding the right questions is about knowing and connecting with ourselves and the students we teach. The logical next question is, then, how can we as teachers stay connected with ourselves and our responses and become aware of the triggers that help us stay in or fall out of connection with our students?

To begin, teachers must regularly experience ourselves as learners. It is important to know what it feels like to be a reader, a writer, a mathematician, a scientist, an artist, and an athlete. In remembering both the vulnerability and the exhilaration that learners experience, teachers can be more attuned to the students' world. Similarly, assuming a learning stance assists teachers in recognizing our own ways of knowing and the ways in which these approaches both resonate and clash with those of our students.

When we begin to see ourselves as well as the students we teach, we begin to recognize and articulate the connection/ disconnection dance in our classrooms. Kayla, a first-year high school Spanish teacher and a graduate student, recounted a recent episode in which her capacity to see herself and her students helped her address a moment when the connection between her and her students had deteriorated dramatically. In many ways, it was a common high school scene: a class labeled "difficult" by her colleagues was "out of control." Students were misbehaving; a few had not completed their classwork; the disengaged few were distracting the rest; and Kayla was furious. The situation became so difficult that she had to call security to remove the most disruptive of her students. "I felt like my classroom had spiraled out of control," Kayla recounted. "The students had lost respect for me, and I, in turn, was behaving like I had lost respect for them."

That evening, she arrived at our graduate seminar frustrated and unsure how to reengage her class. Coincidentally, that evening, I gathered my students into a tight circle to conduct a midsemester review, in which we reflected on our functioning as a group, our learning environment, and ways that the structure of the course both supported and hindered our learning.

Kayla went home that night and considered her options. Could she bring her students into a similar circle? Could she listen to what her students had to say about her class? Could she ask what helped them learn and what got in their way? Bravely, she entered class the next day, moved the chairs and desks from line formation into a horseshoe, and began a conversation with her students. Her students were stunned to be included in a conversation about how the structure and climate of the class needed to be changed. Kayla took "pages of notes" during this meeting and returned to class the next day with a "new plan of how class would run."

The students were surprised to have their ideas included in the changes Kayla made. As Kayla implemented the changes that she and the students had co-constructed, the climate of the class shifted dramatically. "We still struggle every now and then," Kayla said, "but the respect that we have gained for each other has completely changed the classroom environment."

Kayla's story teaches us a number of lessons. Teachers need reflective opportunities—such as meeting with a community of peers, keeping a reflective journal, or participating in mentoring conversations—to help us reflect on our classroom practice, think about the aspects of self we bring to the classroom, and understand our ways of connecting and disconnecting with students.[19] This kind of reflective thinking allows us to gain insight into our identity and practice as teachers and allows us to take restorative action. Finally, in listening closely to her students' needs, opinions, and ideas and taking action that implemented their thinking, Kayla's response was strong, conveying deep respect for her students. She was able to reconnect with her students, thereby reopening the class as a place of learning.

Creating Regular, Dependable, and Responsive Practices

The students in this study teach us that having a voice and being heard are necessary but not sufficient. Students also require clear, nonjudgmental responses from their teachers. As Kayla's story teaches us, this responsiveness is essential in the academic arena as well as in social and emotional domains.

It is tempting to focus on the "best programs" that are designed to help teachers create responsive practices. Indeed, the past two decades have seen the growth of many such programs.[20] These programs have supported many teachers and schools in their efforts to become more closely attuned to the experiences of their students and to engage in genuine dialogue that helps students develop deep understanding of the ideas they construct.

Most central to this discussion, however, are four fundamental principles that guide such practices. First, in responsive practices, teachers need to be engaged in the inquiry at hand so that they are genuinely immersed in the learning process together with students. A pivotal way that teachers and students construct knowledge together is in the creation of curriculum. In such an enterprise, shared mission and focus support a vibrant classroom relationship. When teachers and students join together in defining what is worth knowing—the key task in creating curriculum—they engage in meaningful work that reflects the content and concepts they both value.[21] In the collaborative defining of valuable knowledge, teachers and students create curriculum that not only is deemed useful by the students but also incorporates the very ways in which they understand the world.

In my early work at the Terrace School, my first and second graders were involved in a study of community. Building on a curriculum originally designed at the Bank Street School for Children,[22] the children were constructing a city inside our classroom, replete with buildings such as supermarkets, schools, and stores made out of wooden crates as well as miniature figures who "lived" in the city, ran the services, and purchased the plasticene food and clothing that was carefully made by the storekeepers. As the children completed the construction of the city and were preparing for the two weeks during which they were to "live" in the city, a group of children insisted that the city would be much more authentic if there were lights in the buildings. My co-teacher Rosie and I asked them what they would need to make that happen, and a lively discussion ensued about batteries, bulbs, wires, and circuits. This discussion launched a study of electricity in which the central concepts were explored, hypothesized, tested, and finally applied in wiring the city. The study of electricity had not been part of our intended curriculum but stemmed from the children's interests and emerging understandings about the services that community life requires. The electricity study was one of our most animated science investigations because the questions underlying its inception grew out of our collective study.

The second facet of responsive practices focuses on creating "air time" in the classroom for sharing the thoughts, connections, and associations that regularly happen when children learn something new. Indeed, it is this kind of sharing that can provide the seeds for jointly constructed curriculum. In her landmark essay "The Having of Wonderful Ideas," Eleanor Duckworth argues that the essence of intellectual development is the opportunity to have "wonderful ideas"—that is, ideas students generate out of their experiences.[23] Whether this articulation of children's thinking process occurs when teachers ask students to articulate the multiple ways they solve a mathematics problem or when teachers regularly ask students what they notice when engaged in a scientific exploration, the message is the same: creating ample space for children's articulations of their wonderings and ideas.

Third, responsive practices allow multiple ways of solving problems and ample room for disagreement. I witnessed an exquisite example of this when I was conducting the early phases of the research for this book.[24] In a first/second grade classroom at the Terrace School, Rosie, a veteran teacher at the school, called the children to the rug for a "community meeting."[25] She asked them to think about these questions: How do you become a friend? How do you work out problems with friends? Rosie was asking these questions because she had noticed an increase in playground squabbles. Slowly, the children began talking about trouble on the soccer field and at the monkey bars. In quiet and attentive tones, the children offered reasons for the trouble, sometimes objecting to the perspectives of their classmates. Acknowledging the varying points of view, Rosie asked the children for strategies for solving problems as they come up. One girl, Andrea, suggested that the children should first try to solve a problem on their own, but if they had trouble they should call a teacher. The children all chimed in with suggestions for what to do before calling a teacher. Suresh quietly reminded his classmates that if there is "serious trouble," it is important to call a teacher. Rosie remarked that she had noticed that different children have different feelings about when a teacher is needed and that it is important for each child to know when things are getting out of hand. The children were watching Rosie closely, as if they were trying to figure out whether they knew what that point was for them.

This story stands out in my mind because in creating a community meeting forum, Rosie was creating a sacred space for acknowledging and building the community of the class. In asking the questions as she did, she offered the children the opportunity to voice their experience from whatever vantage point they held, to respectfully disagree, to think about their individual needs, and to collectively solve problems that affected them as a group. This classroom structure communicated to the children the strong message that the classroom is a place to learn about negotiating relationships and that teachers and students together are responsible for recognizing, addressing, and solving the complexities that accompany developing relationships.

Fourth and finally, responsive practices must include opportunities for teachers and students to share impressions and interpretations of students' learning and to co-construct reflections on the learning process. This lesson has been driven home time and again by a gifted sixth-grade teacher, Ron Berger, from Shutesbury, Massachusetts. In his compelling monograph *A Culture of Quality,* Ron advocates for the centrality of formative assessment practices such as portfolios, self-assessment, and community critique.[26] In each of these assessment practices, Ron and his students construct standards of excellence, identify criteria for good work, and confer in assessing the evidence of learning in student work. In this way, the notion of standards is organic to their classroom system, inextricably linked to the learning in the class, and part of an evolving conversation between Ron and the students.

This kind of ongoing conversation between teachers and students about their understanding of student learning is key to building a trustworthy relational context. These conversations are integrally woven into the fabric of school life at the Terrace School and as such made the school an opportune setting for investigating the dynamics of the relational context. From Rosie's first/ second grade class to Maya, Gabe, Sharon, José, Abby, Emily, and Becky's sixth-grade class, all students in the school engage in regular reflection on their learning and on their work with their teachers and peers. This engagement ranges from informal conversations with their teachers to the structured weekly reflection that occurs each Friday throughout the entire school; from daily reflections on their learning to end-of-the-year portfolio reviews conducted by students, parents, and teachers together. The students at the Terrace School engage in regular conversations with their teachers about their learning, sharing standards for good work, formulating problem-solving strategies, and creating a context for getting, in José's words, "all the help" they need.

As the students tell us in this book, such sharing is not an uncomplicated process; yet in the end, these graduating sixth graders are remarkably articulate about their learning, the knowledge they trust, the knowledge they do not trust, what they can say, and what they cannot say. They have grown up in a school that values their words, that asks them to speak, and that inquires when silence creeps in. The school places this kind of interactive assessment culture at the center of its relational context.

Creating Learning Environments That Support Teachers' Ability to Know Their Students

In examining the nature of the teaching-learning relationship, I have referred many times to David Hawkins's triangulated model of I, Thou, and It, which focuses on the teacher, the student, and the subject matter.[27] Carol Rodgers and Sharon Feiman-Nemser have added an essential component to the model, describing a circle that encompasses the triangle, reflecting the context that so profoundly shapes school culture and this triarchic relationship.[28] When I teach a graduate seminar called "Understanding Learning and Teaching,"[29] my students and I spend a good portion of the semester investigating this triangle, trying to understand the complexity of the teacher-student-content relationship. We end the semester by trying to define the forces of context that create the circle around the triangle. In a brainstorming session in which students construct a definition of "context," I draw a triangle on the board that is circumscribed by a circle. I record all their concepts of context on the circle as they speak (see Figure 8.1).

Around the circle, we place words like "time," "budget," "diversity," "school board," "standardized testing," "administration," "facilities," "books," "parent relationships," "tenure," "teacher next door," "mentor," "teaching trend of the moment," "metal detectors,"

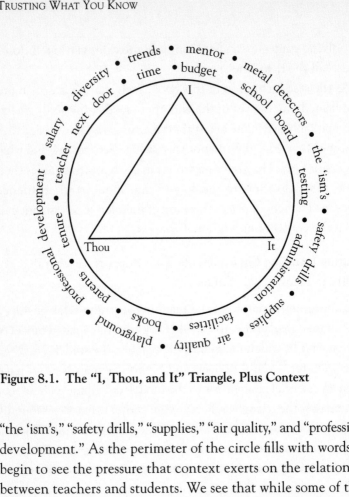

Figure 8.1. The "I, Thou, and It" Triangle, Plus Context

"the 'ism's," "safety drills," "supplies," "air quality," and "professional development." As the perimeter of the circle fills with words, we begin to see the pressure that context exerts on the relationship between teachers and students. We see that while some of these pressures strengthen the triangle, others threaten its structure.

Interestingly, the students in this book speak little about the ways that the culture of school shapes their relationships with their teachers and peers. Abby is a noted exception to this when she claims a stance that is in opposition to what she understands to be the "Terrace way." The reasons for this marked lack of discussion could be attributed to the fact that I did not ask the students directly about the ways they saw the school culture supporting and impeding their relationships. Another possibility is that the students saw me, a former teacher at the school, as part of the context and therefore did not feel free to comment or critique in this way. Alternatively, if they did view me as part of the context, perhaps they assumed that I shared their basic understanding of the school and that it was therefore unnecessary to state it.

While the students in this study are quiet about their school culture, the teachers in my seminars are well aware of the pragmatic considerations that affect their capacity to develop genuine relationships with their students. These factors include class size, schedule, physical environment, school structure, and issues of diversity. If establishing and nurturing teacher-student relationships is important, then class sizes must be manageable, so that teachers and students can actually get to know one another "in fundamental ways."[30] Likewise, teachers and administrators need to consider whether the school schedule permits the extended conversations and investigation that would provide the shared focus that McDermott cites as prerequisite for trusting relationships in schools.[31] For example, when children make a transition from one teacher to another every forty minutes, what kinds of conversations can be had within that construct? In addition, to create extended investigations, students and teachers need access to the physical space and materials that facilitate these explorations. Similarly, when classroom teachers do not experience the arts with their students, leaving this work to specialists, they lose opportunities to know their students fully. Gabe and Maya demonstrate the central role that athletics and the arts play in their capacity to know. A teacher who does not see children in these contexts is not seeing the modalities through which they come to know the world.[32] Finally, issues of diversity—that is, issues of race, culture, class, gender, sexual identity, the "ism's" of our society—must be attended to in an open, ongoing, and integrated way in order to create a trusting context in which all voices are invited.

In considering the factors of school context and culture, it is tempting to dismiss them as out of teachers' control. By and large, teachers do not make the decisions about structures such as class size and scheduling. This fact in and of itself is ironic, because these are the factors that most affect the quality of teachers' work. Yet these issues are raised here because teachers are the adults with the most direct knowledge of and experience with students. If teachers were able to act on our knowledge of students, how could we change the culture of schools?

Taking Action

What does it mean to act on what we know about our students? What stops us? How can we overcome these obstacles? These are the core questions that sit with me daily as I engage teachers and researchers in university and school settings. Together with my students, I have come to understand that acting on what we know requires first and foremost that teachers acknowledge that we construct real knowledge about the relational aspects of children's learning on a daily basis. Hand in hand with this recognition is the articulation of this knowledge and, ultimately, trusting what we know. In my ongoing work with teachers in professional development contexts as well as in the graduate program in which I teach and advise, I have come to understand how difficult it can be for teachers to assume a relational stance. This stance is often at odds with test mandates, standardized curriculum, and rigid state-determined standards. Often, teachers justifiably fear retribution from their school and their district if they choose to spend curricular time on community-building work, on responding to children's emotional and social concerns, or on developing curriculum that stems from children's interests.

When teachers place students' needs and their relationship with their students at the center of the curriculum, teachers are taking a political stand. At this point in history, this is a stand that resists the culture of standardization. Perhaps this is the hardest stand to take in the current political climate. It is the culture of standardization, however, that poses the biggest threat to the construction of healthy relationships in schools.

Challenging the Culture of Standardization: A Call to Action

The standardized culture of education today suggests that "objective measures," such as high-stakes testing, and standardized curriculum will help students learn more effectively. Yet the very measures espoused by politicians, policymakers, and researchers as the silver bullet to save education are systematically undermining the foundational relationships in the classroom, thereby eroding the most central pillar in the knowledge-building enterprise.

This systematic attack on school relationships is alarming from both the teaching and learning perspectives. For teachers, the standardized curriculum and assessments that flood their classrooms create numerous obstacles to their efforts to both know their students and act on the knowledge they have. One veteran kindergarten teacher, after a session of the doctoral seminar I teach called "The Relational Context of Teaching and Learning," aptly reflected: "I'm thinking, in the light of increasing standards-based work in the classroom *and* the need to justify every moment spent in the classroom with children, about how 'relationship' is being trivialized, marginalized.

It's my hope that we will not only explore the relational context of teaching but also the instantiation of the relational in a context that has become hostile (or, at best, neutral) towards the relational/affective/social spheres [of the classroom]."[33]

When faced with a curriculum that mandates teaching a certain page on a certain date, often teachers cannot make curricular decisions based on what they think their students need. When teachers lose the power to act on what they know, their knowledge loses value, and their desire to know what they know about their students can wane. When a teacher knows that Susie needs to focus on the concept of subtraction, yet the curriculum mandates instruction of multiplication, what is a teacher to do with this knowledge? How does she build her relationship with Susie when she cannot act on what she knows? In short, the culture of standardization creates a culture of teaching in which teachers' knowledge loses its currency.

As for students, the culture of standardization tells them that their perspectives on their learning has little value in the classroom. Their communications with their teachers do not matter, because their teachers do not have the time or power to act on this knowledge. Students' individual needs and desires take second place to preparing for tests and meeting learning objectives determined by adults far removed from their classroom. The culture of standardization interrupts students' capacity to voice their understanding of their learning, because in a standardized culture, this understanding has little value. The most alarming aspect of this culture is the interruption of communication between teachers and students. Without communication, teachers and students reduce their capacity to know one another and to enter into a relationship that facilitates learning on all of their parts.

Because the standardized culture is so pervasive in our educational system today, the words expressed by the students in this volume are an urgent call to action. It is a call to resist the pressures of standardization that tear at the fabric of relationships. The students tell us that they need these trusting relationships as a prerequisite for building knowledge that is robust, that is secure, and that can be communicated. Without such relationships, their burgeoning knowledge is at risk. The students' stories in this volume tell us that in order to construct trustworthy knowledge, their classrooms must be places where trusting relationships are built. The dynamics of these relationships—the pressures, the expectations, the pleasures— create a culture in which children determine whether they can trust one another and their teachers. Within the web of relationships, students learn to trust themselves as learners, as actors in their classroom, and in the world. Students also learn to read these relationships and determine to what extent it is safe to bring their knowledge to them. In essence, classrooms are laboratories for learning about and working through the complexities of relationships. The call to action asks us to preserve these essential relational underpinnings of classroom life.

Finally, the call to action asks teachers to trust what we know about the place of relationships in the learning process. Trusting what we know urges us to recognize the inherently political nature of teaching. Trusting what we know is risky and requires courage. Yet these risks are worth taking both for the sake of our students and for the sake of our own integrity. Taking such a relational stand in the classroom teaches our students, colleagues, and parents that trust, honesty, and the construction of knowledge are at the core of the journey of education.

Notes

1. Hawkins, 1974.

2. Miller & Stiver, 1997.

3. See Kohn, 1992, for a thorough discussion of competition in the classroom. Also see Roeser, Eccles, & Sameroff, 2000, for a review of the research demonstrating the deleterious effects of a competitive environment in student learning and socioemotional functioning. See also Krechevsky, 2001, for a discussion of group learning and knowledge construction.

4. Charney, 2002.

5. See especially Paley, 1986a, 1990, 1991, 2004.

6. Paley, 1986b, p. 124.

7. Paley, 1986b, p. 131.

8. Brown & Gilligan, 1992.

9. Schultz, 2003.

10. Schultz, 2003, p. 16.

11. Perrone, 1991.

12. Himley & Carini, 2000, p. vi.

13. Carini, 1979, 2001; Cohen, Stern, & Balaban, 1997; Haberman, 2000; Himley & Carini, 2000; Seidel, 1998.

14. Rodgers, 2002a, 2002b.

15. Seidel, 1998.

16. Tappan, 2001.

17. Examples of interpretive communities are study groups and inquiry groups (Weinbaum and others, 2004) such as the Philadelphia Teachers Learning Collaborative (Abu El-Haj, 2003), the Teaching Boys Study Group (Raider-Roth, 2003), the Parker Study Group (Raider-Roth and others, 2003); conference groups in the teacher education programs at Bank Street College in New York (Haberman, 2000; Nager & Shapiro, 2000), descriptive review groups (Cochran-Smith & Lytle, 1993; Himley & Carini, 2000), collaborative assessment groups (Seidel, 1998) and evidence groups (Project Zero, 2001).

18. See Rodgers 2002b.

19. For examples of such practices, see Abu El-Haj 2003; Strieb, 1985; Cochran-Smith & Lytle, 1993.

20. Examples of such programs include Responsive Classroom (Charney, 2002); Developing Mathematical Ideas (Shifter, Bastable, & Russell, 1999); Writing and Reading Workshop (Atwell, 1998; Calkins, 1986, 2001); and Teaching for Understanding (Blythe, 1997; Wiske, 1998).

21. Cuffaro, 1995, 2000.

22. Gold, 1978.

23. Duckworth, 1987.

24. Raider-Roth, 2004.

25. For more information on community meetings and morning meetings, see Charney, 2002, and Kriete, 2002.

26. Berger, 1996.

27. Hawkins, 1974.

28. Feiman-Nemser, 2003. Rodgers, 2002a, 2002b.

29. This course was codeveloped with Carol Rodgers. This discussion grows out of our many conversations about theory and practice of this course.

30. Harriet Cuffaro, personal communication, January 16, 1999.

31. McDermott, 1977.

32. Perrone, 1998.

33. Eric Gidseg, personal communication, September 15, 2003.

Epilogue:
The Heart of the Onion

Spring 2004: Twelve years after Sharon, Maya, Abby, Gabe, José, Emily, and Becky walked into my classroom as first and second graders, and six years after their interviews and their graduation from the Terrace School, they are now poised to graduate from high school and set off for college. This spring they gathered once again, in the halls of the Terrace School and in the living room of Sharon's house. I had initiated these gatherings, asking them if they would like to read the chapters of this book in which their interviews are discussed.

Four years before, I had invited the students to come to the school to read their transcripts, but there was a power to the current visit that was palpably different from the earlier one. Perhaps it was the reality that their words were actually going to become part of a book. Perhaps it was my intimacy with their words; although they had grown into adulthood, leaving these interviews and the halls of the Terrace School long ago, I continued to live with them as twelve-year-olds. In a sense, in my mind, they had never grown up, so seeing these striking young adults shocked me back to the reality that these children had grown.

And yet when they read their chapters, they recognized themselves. Many of them responded that they still believed what they had said. Some of them remarked that they had a hard time understanding their words, but when they read my interpretations, they could see themselves clearly. Gabe commented how true these analyses were for him still, on the eve of leaving for college. Similarly, Emily reflected that issues of "lying versus telling the truth" have always been ones that she thinks about. In reading the chapters, she commented on how she had "applied that idea to my life *now*" and compared it to "how I applied it then." Maya reflected on how much she had changed yet how glad she was that I had captured a part of her life that had seemed to go underground. Abby, reading Chapters Six and Seven with great care, commented that she thought my analysis rang true but was not sharp enough when it came to assessment. She reminded me that assessment is all about comparison and that unless I am explicit about this point, readers would not understand the complex thinking that is required for students and teachers in the assessment process. Becky, in reflecting on her comments about teachers' expectations, affirmed her interpretation. Sitting with her father, she said she thinks that it is even more true now and that the more she tries to meet teachers' expectations, the less self-confidence she has. Sharon commented that the "I poems" seem to get at the heart of what they were saying about themselves.

These conversations with the students provided the most important validity check on this study. Not only could they recognize themselves, but they could see how aspects of their ideas about trust, truth, and knowing still held strong in their lives. They freely critiqued my interpretations, offering extensions, modifications, and additions to mine. They also reminded me when I got the facts wrong—such as eye color or their exact age at the time of the interview. Perhaps the most powerful validation of the study, resonating with what Elliot Eisner terms "consensual validation," was the students' statements that when they could not understand their own words, they felt that the interpretations I offered helped them to see themselves.[1] To my relief, the interpretations brought their understandings into focus rather than obscurity.

And so the onion continues to unfold. Through the research relationships that set the stage for this study, we have seen the students' relationships with their learning, their teachers, and their peers. And in examining the students' understandings of these relationships, we can see the interplay between these connections and the many forces that shape the students' capacity to learn. We gain glimpses of family, school culture, teachers' presence, peer interactions, and images of relational learning selves that grow and evolve over time. In the unfolding of these layers and at the essential core, we can see how students' trust in self and trust in others are essentially intertwined.

Note

1. Eisner, 1998.

Appendix:
Listening Closely: Discovery
and the Research Relationship

Discovery Research: A Relational Enterprise

When I entered the territory of children's relational understandings of school, I stepped into a landscape that did not have a well-defined map. While researchers, as I have noted, have described points of tension, little was understood about children's relational knowledge of schooling. The early phases of this research suggested that this process was to be "a journey of discovery,"[1] a journey into a land without roads, street signs, or traffic signals. Over time, I came to understand that the central mission of this study was to identify and record the defining features of the landscape, making future expeditions possible. This was to be "discovery research."[2] Most important, I learned that the process of discovery is an inherently relational process. That is, to construct new knowledge means developing and maintaining relationships with the students, my questions, the research process, and the data.

The process of discovery meant being open to possibilities I did not expect, observing closely, questioning the obvious, and listening as carefully as possible. Learning to listen to the children of this study proved to be the most important and most difficult part of this process of discovery and being in relationship. Indeed, learning to listen meant attending fully to the students' experiences, keeping close track of all their stories, questions, reactions, and ideas. It also meant being attuned to my own responses to their thinking and my feelings about the issues that arose. In addition, as described in the Prologue and elsewhere, the parallel process phenomenon often presented itself in the interviews, with a variety of dynamics arising between the students and me. Keeping an eye on the research relationship was therefore a crucial component of the listening. By paying close attention to the students' thinking, my own reactions, and the dynamics of the relationships, I aimed to plot the major features of the landscape that both the students and I confronted, which in turn raised new questions and suggested new paths to explore.

Discovery research is an approach that affords the opportunity to follow one's questions, uncover terrain provoked by those questions, refine the questions, continue in the excavation of the landscape, and refine the questions even more. A certainty in discovery research is that both research questions and interpretations continue to evolve and change as the research process continues and deepens. The analysis presented in this volume is a resting point in a dynamic process. It is a moment to gather up the evidence collected thus far in order to paint a picture of this landscape. This analysis will allow me, other researchers, and teachers to frame the next set of questions and continue the journey.

Two years after interviewing the students for this book, I met with many of them to show them the transcripts of their interviews. In doing so, I rediscovered the extraordinary power of growth, change, and continuity in their lives. As Maya read her transcripts, she whispered, "I've changed so much." Although she could recognize the girl speaking on the pages, she had moved to a new place in her life. José captured the sense of seeing himself in the past while also seeing himself in the present when he said, "it brings back a part of you." Indeed, these interviews are but a small part of these children's evolving and changing lives, and this research should be read with this in mind.

Discovering the Questions: Attending to the Researcher as a Relational Learner

Discovery research invites and encourages the researcher to permit and track the evolution of the focusing research questions. As in all careful qualitative research, the assumption is that research questions are not static and that they will change as discoveries are made during the research process.[3] The distinguishing feature of discovery research is the careful tracking of the growth and evolution of the questions. These changes can be seen as data in and of themselves because they mark points in time when the knowledge shared in the research process shapes the process itself. This juncture reveals the relational quality of this process. As the researcher begins to hear the responses of the participant, the questions begin to shift. As the researcher listens closely and shifts the questions, the participants' responses deepen. As the participant begins to make the researcher's questions her own—that is, reframe them to tap into genuine curiosities of her own—the researcher's questions can shift again. In this recursive process, the reciprocal nature of the research relationship is seen.

My questions unfolded and emerged in response to talking with the children and repeatedly listening to their narratives and stories. When I began the study, I asked the following questions:

- How do students understand the ways in which the relational dynamics of self-assessment work facilitate and disrupt their capacity to trust what they know?

- What aspects of school relationships are most important to students when thinking about self-assessment work?

- What aspects of school relationships do students believe help them to trust their knowledge?

- What aspects of school relationships do students believe make it difficult for them to trust their knowledge?

As I followed these questions with the students, I was able to see that trusting self and trusting others were highly interrelated processes. I then sought to understand how these processes of trust worked in the classroom. As I began to see that in their self-assessment work, students were actively suppressing aspects of their knowledge, depending on their audience, I began to ask whether this selective disclosure caused students to lose track of or lose faith in what they knew. I studied the interviews, searching for evidence of the interrelationship between trusting self and trusting others. In the process of collecting this evidence, I began to see the politics of the students' actions and see their acts of resistance and participation as a reflection of their capacity to see and assess the genuine nature of the motives of the adults in their midst.[4] I found myself asking questions about educational practice and the direct and indirect messages that our practices communicate to students about teachers' willingness to be in a genuine relationship with them. I returned to the interviews yet again, looking for the evidence of answers to these questions.

The evolution of the research questions in discovery research is a recursive process that requires the researcher to listen carefully for the ever-deepening meaning contained within the interviewee's narratives. This kind of listening requires full attention and a commitment to being present with the person interviewed and the stories told. As in teaching, the rewards of discovery research are immense because the process takes us a step closer to seeing the full humanity and capacity of the people who teach and inform us in the research process.[5]

The Interview Process: Attending to the Researcher-Participant Relationship

Recognizing the relational context of the interview process is a core element of the research methodology used in this study. That is, the knowledge communicated and constructed in the interview process is embedded in the quality of relationship between the interviewer and interviewee. In my interviews with Maya and Gabe in particular, the children's willingness to talk about the ideas most important to them hinged on their ability to see that I was truly listening and attempting to view the world the way they viewed it. When I tried to squeeze their understandings into my worldview, they stepped back, seeing that I was not ready to step into their perspective. It is important to keep in mind, always, that the knowledge shared, the aspects of self revealed, are contextualized by the research relationship and the questions we ask.

Assuming a relational stance in the interview process requires attention to the words, gestures, facial expressions, and body language of the interviewee, as well as an attentiveness to one's own responses, associations, and emotions. In this study, two clinical interviewing approaches supported this stance. The first, rooted in Piagetian clinical interviewing/exploration methods, focuses on the way that the interviewee makes meaning of ideas, words, and terminology.[6] It is a genuine attempt to "understand the learners' understanding."[7] For example, I asked students to explain specific terms, such as "confidence" and "respect," being sure not to assume a shared understanding. The second approach is a voice-centered, relational one, drawing on the psychological foundations of the "Listening Guide," which is described in more detail in the next section. This approach centers on the ways that the learner constructs the meaning embedded in her life experiences.[8] The interviews were semistructured and open-ended, allowing me to follow students' associations in response to my questions and at the same time focus on the key aspects of relationship. This methodology helped me understand the complexity of the students' ideas while remaining attuned to the relational dynamics of the interview. As part of the interview protocol, I checked my interpretations with the students throughout the interview with questions or comments such as "So what I hear you saying is . . . " and "Am I understanding you correctly if I were to say . . . ?"[9] If necessary, I checked as to whether they were telling me their opinions or what they thought I wanted to hear by asking questions such as "Do you really feel that way?" and "Is that what you think you are supposed to say?" These questions served as validity checks in that they offered me and the students the opportunity to hear how I understood their ideas and to correct misunderstandings.[10]

Listening Closely to the Data: Listening to the Children

I analyzed the interviews by using the "Listening Guide."[11] This voice-centered, relational method involves multiple "listenings," or readings, of the interview text in order to disentangle the many themes raised, to hear the multiple voices expressed in the interview, and to become clear about one's stance as a researcher—one's biases, attitudes, questions, and confusions. I chose this relational method of analysis because my research questions seek students' understandings of the functioning of relationships in the classroom. As I discussed earlier, the interview is a relational process, requiring a method of analysis that can track the dynamics of relationship that the students describe in regard to their classroom as well as the dynamics that arise in the interview. In addition, my research questions asked students to share with me their thinking—or their internal conversations—about how they responded to the ways that work and relationships were embedded in school. In seeking to understand these internal conversations, I required a method of analysis that would allow me to hear the intricacies and various voices in such conversations.

The Listening Guide requires that each interview be listened to at least four distinct times. In the first listening, the goal is to pay close attention to the stories that the students tell and to create a detailed outline of the salient issues that arise. Understanding the main story lines, or the "plot," is a central feature of this listening. I also listen closely for the continuity and change of the narrative positions (first-, second-, and third-person stance) that the students used to tell their stories. Emerging themes are traced, categorized, and carefully recorded. For each student, I maintain a master list that in which I record all the themes mentioned throughout the students' interviews, track the subthemes, and note the location of each reference. I also mark the sections of narrative that need closer listening.

A central feature of the first listening is paying careful attention to the "silences," or issues that go unmentioned. For example, in this research, I was careful to note when students did not raise issues related to honesty and disclosure or did not want to attend to these issues. While these issues may not have been equally salient for all the students, their absence in our conversation communicated a powerful message as well. I took care to note the silences and collected related evidence that might explain these moments of quiet. Similarly, I tracked my own silences. For example, I am aware that I did not ask students about their cultural, racial, ethnic, or religious backgrounds or knowledge. The students also did not raise this key way of knowing the world. I recognize that I also did not ask about issues of gender. I am aware that my silence may have contributed to their silence. Perhaps both the students and I viewed these issues as assumed knowledge between us because of our long-standing relationship. Perhaps the intensity of the conversations stopped me from raising issues that I know are deeply complex for fear of overwhelming myself and the students. Wishing that I could now ask the students about these ways of knowing, I note these silences in order to alert us as teachers and researchers to the absence or presence of these issues in our conversations with students.[12]

In addition, the first listening requires the interviewer to be mindful and keep track of her own responses, questions, and confusions. This "reader's response" is a key aspect of the first reading because it urges the researcher to carefully separate her own responses from that of her subject. This diminishes the possibility of using the subject's voice to tell the researcher's story.[13] The reader's response is an important tool in tracking the interactions in the interview that may parallel or represent the issues that are discussed in the interview. By acknowledging and examining the interviewing relationship, I am able to learn from the tensions, the moments that felt in sync, and the times when I felt lost. Because the central question of this study examines the way that relationships affect students' knowing, it is essential to pay close attention to the interviewing relationship and how it affects both my own and the students' capacity to talk and think.

In tracking my own responses and listening for silences, I become not only a "responsive" listener but also a "resisting" one.[14] As a responsive listener, I try to enter the students' experiences, reflecting on both the ways in which they express their ideas and how I hear them. As a resisting listener, I listen for ideas and meanings that are counter to the dominant culture or, in this case, counter to the students' perceptions of the school's assumptions regarding relationship, self-assessment work, trust, and knowledge.[15]

The second listening focuses on how the students describe themselves, their knowledge, and their work. In the second listening, I pay close attention to the voice of the self, which is often expressed in the voice of the first-person "I." By tracing the "I" statements in the interview, the interviewer is able to hear the thoughts, desires, wishes, needs, conflicts, and silences that are articulated in the first-person voice. Because an understanding of the students' relationship to their work and their own knowledge is central to this study, this second listening is a fundamental feature of my analysis. As a relational method, the second listening is a crucial step in allowing the interviewer to enter the world of the interviwee.[16] When I listen to a series of "I" statements, I gain another level of understanding of the students' experiences of school that I do not hear when I listen for themes and stories. I hear how the processes of knowing, learning, and trusting are spoken in the first-person voice. With this understanding, I can hear the psychological depth of the students' stories.[17]

An essential aspect of the second listening is actually drawing out the "I" statements from the narrative. In practice, this means that as I read the transcripts, I underline each "I" statement (for example, "I know," "I want," "I can," "I think") with a purple colored pencil. I then create what has been termed an "I poem"—a series of "I" statements, recorded in sequence from a distinct paragraph or story in the interview. Often the "I" voice is in conversation with a "you" voice or a "they" voice, illuminating the students' internal conversations. When this happens, I trace the second- or third-person voices as well (using green for "you" and brown for "they"), often creating dialogues or conversations. For example, in this excerpt from Jon's interview, he is speaking about his learning:

> To say, you know, I am learning something, you know, *because you might not be* [*pause*] [*there is a seriousness about that phrase in his voice*], and usually you are when you have a teacher or something, but I mean sometimes it is a review for people, and sometimes you just gotta, you know, maybe it'll seem weird, and you'll think you're really not learning anything, and you *know* you're not learning anything, just still gotta say I *am*. I am learning something, and I'm gonna learn something, and I'm gonna learn more and more and more.

When I extract the "I" and "you" voices to hear them clearly, the narrative sounds like this:

I	You
I am learning	You know
	You know
	You might not be
	Usually you are
	You have
I mean	
	You just gotta
	You know
	You'll think
	You're really not learning
	You know
	you're not learning
I am	
I am learning	
I'm gonna learn	
I'm gonna learn	

Listening in this way allows me to hear Jon's internal struggle, as represented by the "I" and the "you," regarding his desire to learn and his acute concern that he is not learning. The tension between the "I" and the "you" is palpable. The "I poems" and "voice poems" are central to this analysis because they draw out the internal conversations so that they are audible and the nuances can readily be seen. Thus, examples of these "voice poems" occur throughout the individual stories in the book.

The third and fourth listenings focus on the prevailing "contrapuntal" voices in the text. I have found it useful to think of these listenings as an effort to elicit the complexity of the overarching tensions in a narrative. I seek to track how prevailing themes in the text both resonate and clash with one another and, in doing so, to locate the dynamic tensions between them. These contrapuntal listenings invite the researcher's innovative and creative thinking. At this stage of the research, the researcher has identified key themes and has begun to hear the tensions within. The researcher can now name these tensions and begin to listen to them specifically and in depth. In this research, the contrapuntal listenings focused on the variety of ways in which the students talk about relationships.[18] I paid close attention to the aspects of relationships that students believed helped them learn or know and the aspects of relationships that obstructed their knowing. Specifically, I listened to the ways that students spoke of knowing and not knowing, trust and mistrust, and connection and disconnection. As I read and listened to the transcripts, I underlined each set of tensions with a particular colored pencil, tracking the ebb and flow of their presence in the narrative.

In order to render a coherent synthesis of my understandings and interpretations, I found it most useful to focus on two major themes in regard to which the students described their experiences of these tensions. I chose the themes of telling the truth and audience as focal points for examining the tensions in the narratives. Tracing these thematic tensions, I followed the threads of students' feelings of honesty in self-assessment work, students' experiences of trusting and mistrusting their knowledge in school, and students' experiences of feeling connected to and disconnected from their teachers and peers. In watching how these threads converged and remained distinct, I aimed to build an understanding of the ways in which the relational dynamics of self-assessment contribute to students' capacity to trust their knowledge. My purpose in the third and fourth listenings was to describe, as closely as possible, the features, nuances, and mechanics of these tensions.

The final step in the Listening Guide Process is to create a narrative synthesis that brings all four listenings together. Sometimes this is referred to as a summary or analysis of the four listenings.

I employ the term "synthesis" because the central task in this step is to bring together the variety of insights gleaned throughout the listenings to construct a coherent analysis, a coherent story. This is a challenging and key aspect of the process, for this is when the researcher begins to articulate his or her understanding of the narrative. The synthesis stage asks the researcher to form an interpretation of the interviewee's words, ideas, and stories. This is a heavy responsibility indeed.[19]

The Listening Guide provides a creative and flexible map for listening to the narrative at hand and coming into relationship with the text and with the speakers of the text. Its goal is to elicit the complexity embedded within a text in an effort not to reduce the tensions to discrete categories but to raise up the beauty of the human psyche and assist the researcher in navigating the bumpy terrain of relational life.

Listening to the Data: Attending to the Strength of the Interpretations

The validity of this analysis, or the strength and veracity of the themes, questions, and interpretations, was checked in a number of ways. First, by having two interviews for analysis, I was able to trace how the students' opinions evolved and changed and follow the threads that remained constant in both interviews. Tracking the constants and the contradictions gave me insight into the bedrock assumptions and feelings that the students held as well as the dilemmas that they faced.

Second, selections of the interviews and analyses were read by members of an "interpretive community."[20] The community consisted of two people who had familiarity with the Listening Guide and two people who were acquainted with the issues of self-assessment, relationship, and schooling.[21] In this way, I could assess whether I had located issues of relationship that other teachers and researchers could also readily identify. Likewise, I could check interpretations that were informed by the Listening Guide with others who have experience creating "the trail of evidence" that the guide demands.[22] Both points of agreement and points of disagreement were important information regarding the validity of my interpretations.

Finally, in an effort to check my interpretations with the students, I offered them an opportunity to read the transcripts of their interviews, to ask questions, and, ultimately, to read and respond to the chapters and sections of this book in which their interviews are discussed. As I have described in the Epilogue, these conversations were essential to validating the interpretations offered herein.[23]

Limitations

Because it focuses on the thoughts of a small group of predominantly European American children, this study is clearly limited in scope. My goal is not to make generalizable claims regarding the experiences of all twelve-year-olds engaged in self-assessment. Rather, as a discovery researcher, I attempt to locate the main themes, tensions, provocations, and beliefs that these children hold in regard to the relational aspects of self-assessment work. In drawing out their stories, I highlight aspects of classroom relationships and their impact on reflective classroom practices. As Lawrence-Lightfoot and Davis suggest, in the description of the "particular"—stories, narrative, portraits—we can discover the "universal"—essential aspects of the human experience.[24]

By identifying points of resonance and divergence in the relational landscape drawn by these students, this research method seeks to inform the direction of future study concerning the dynamics of classroom relationships and how such interactions shape children's capacity to engage in self-assessment and, ultimately, to learn and to know. Indeed, I view this research as setting the stage for future studies to examine how children—in a variety of school settings;

who are of varied race, culture, class, and ethnicity; and who have not been my students—understand and articulate issues of trust and knowledge. As discovery research, this study has described the key features of the relational landscape of classroom life, inviting future researchers to continue unearthing the complex terrain of relationships, trust, and knowledge.

Notes

1. Brown & Gilligan, 1992, p. 16.
2. Carol Gilligan generously taught me the terrain of "discovery research," or "discovery phase research." I credit her with this research construct. Carol first used the geographical journey as a metaphor to describe this research process. Her assignment of writing the "Landscape of My Question" in her "Clinical Interviewing" course gave birth to the language of journey—travel, territory, path, and terrain—that is embedded in this study. I am grateful to Carol for this metaphor. Also see Gilligan, Spencer, Weinberg, & Bertsch, 2003, for a discussion of discovery research.
3. Maxwell, 1996.
4. The relational concept of resistance has been well researched and documented; see Brown & Gilligan, 1992, & Rogers, 1993.
5. I credit Patricia F. Carini with the realization that when we look and listen carefully, we are learning about humanity and capacity.
6. For more detail on this approach to clinical interviewing/ exploration, see Duckworth, 1987, 2001, and Piaget, 1929/1969.
7. Duckworth, 1987, p. 83.
8. Gilligan, Spencer, Weinberg, & Bertsch, 2003.
9. Anderson & Jack, 1991.
10. Borland, 1991.
11. Brown and others, 1988; Brown, 1998; Gilligan, Brown, & Rogers, 1990; Brown & Gilligan, 1992; Gilligan, Spencer, Weinberg, & Bertsch, 2003; Jack, 1993; Rogers, Brown, & Tappan, 1993; Taylor, Gilligan, & Sullivan, 1995; Tolman, 2002; Way, 1998.

12. Rogers, 1993.

13. Anderson & Jack, 1991; Brown & Gilligan, 1992; Rogers, 1993.

14. Brown & Gilligan, 1991, 1992.

15. Brown & Gilligan, 1991; Fetterly, 1978.

16. Gilligan, Spencer, Weinberg, & Bertsch, 2003; Brown & Gilligan, 1992.

17. Gilligan, Spencer, Weinberg, & Bertsch, 2003; Brown & Gilligan, 1992; Gilligan, Brown, & Rogers, 1990.

18. Brown & Gilligan, 1992.

19. Gilligan, Spencer, Weinberg, & Bertsch, 2003.

20. Tappan, 2001; Taylor, Gilligan & Sullivan, 1995.

21. Constructing an interpretive community in this way is modeled in Tai, 1999.

22. Taylor, Gilligan, & Sullivan, 1995.

23. Borland, 1991; Eisner, 1998.

24. Lawrence-Lightfoot & Davis, 1997.

References

Abu El-Haj, T. R. (2003). Practicing for equity from the standpoint of the particular: Exploring the work of one urban teacher network. *Teachers College Record 105*(5), 817–845.

Allen, D. (Ed.). (1998). *Assessing student learning.* New York: Teachers College Press.

Anderson, K., & Jack, D. C. (1991). Learning to listen: Interview techniques and analyses. In S. B. Gluck & D. Patai (Eds.), *Women's words: The feminist practice of oral history* (pp. 11–26). New York: Routledge.

Andrade, H. (2003). Teaching the habit of self-assessment. *Journal of the Institute for Democracy and Education, 14*(4), 31–35.

Andrade, H., & Boulay, B. A. (2003). The role of self-assessment in learning to write. *Journal of Educational Research, 97*(1), 21–34.

Atwell, N. (1998). *In the middle.* Portsmouth, NH: Boynton/Cook.

Belenky, M. F., Clinchy, B. M., Goldberger, N. R., & Tarule, J. M. (1986). *Women's ways of knowing.* New York: Basic Books.

Berger, R. (1996). *A culture of quality* (Occasional Paper Series 1). Providence, RI: The Annenberg Institute for School Reform.

Birch, S. H., & Ladd, G. W. (1997). The teacher-child relationship and children's early school adjustment. *Journal of School Psychology 35*(1), 61–79.

Black, P. (1995). *Teachers' assessments and pupils' self-assessments.* Paper presented at the meeting of the National Association for Research in Science Teaching, San Francisco.

Black, P., Harrison, C., Lee, C., Marshall, B., & William, D. (2004). Working inside the black box: Assessment for learning in the classroom. *Phi Delta Kappan, 86*(1), 8–21.

Black, P., & William, D. (1998). Inside the black box: raising standards through classroom assessment. *Phi Delta Kappan, 80*(2), 139–144.

Blythe, T. (1997). *Teaching for understanding guide*. San Francisco: Jossey-Bass.

Borland, K. (1991). "That's not what I said": Interpretive conflict in oral narrative research. In S. B. Gluck & D. Patai (Eds.), *Women's words: The feminist practice of oral history* (pp. 63–76). New York: Routledge.

Brown, L. (1998). *Raising their voices: The politics of girls' anger*. Cambridge, MA: Harvard University Press.

Brown, L. (2003). *Girlfighting: Betrayal and rejection among girls*. New York: New York University Press.

Brown, L. M., Argyris, D., Attanucci, J., Bardige, B., Gilligan, C., Johnston, D. K., Miller, B., Osborne, R., Tappan, M., Ward, J., Wiggins, G., & Wilcox, D. (1988). *A guide to reading narratives of conflict and choice for self and relational voice* (Monograph no. 1). Cambridge, MA: Project on the Psychology of Women and the Development of Girls, Harvard Graduate School of Education.

Brown, L. M., & Gilligan, C. (1991). Listening for voice in narratives of relationships. In M. B. Tappan & M. J. Packer (Eds.), *Narrative and storytelling: Implications for understanding moral development* (pp. 43–61). New Directions for Child Development No. 54. San Francisco: Jossey-Bass.

Brown, L. M., & Gilligan, C. (1992). *Meeting at the crossroads*. New York: Ballantine Books.

Browne, R., & Fletcher, R. (Eds.). (1995). *Boys in schools: Addressing the real issues—behavior, values and relationships*. Sydney, Australia: Finch Press.

Bruce, L. B. (2001). Student self-assessment. *Classroom Leadership, 5*(1). Retrieved February 24, 2004, from http://www.ascd.org/publications/call_lead/200109/bruce.html

Bryk, A. S., & Schneider, B. (2002). *Trust in schools: A core resource for improvement*. New York: Russell Sage Foundation.

Buber, M. (1958). *I and Thou* (2nd ed.). New York: Scribner.

Calkins, L. M. (1986). *The art of teaching writing*. Portsmouth, NH: Heinemann.

Calkins, L. M. (2001). *The art of teaching reading*. New York: Longman.

Carini, P. F. (1979). *The art of seeing and the visibility of the person*. Grand Forks: North Dakota Study Group on Evaluation.

Carini, P. F. (2001). *Starting strong: A different look at children, schools and standards*. New York: Teachers College Press.

Charney, R. (2002). *Teaching children to care* (rev. ed.). Greenfield, MA: Northeast Foundation for Children.

Chu, J. (2000). *Learning what boys know: An observational and interview study with six four-year-old boys*. Unpublished dissertation, Harvard Graduate School of Education, Cambridge, MA.

Cochran-Smith, M., & Lytle, S. L. (1993). *Inside/outside: Teacher research and knowledge*. New York: Teachers College Press.

Cohen, D. H., Stern, V., & Balaban, N. (1997). *Observing and recording the behavior of young children* (4th ed.). New York: Teachers College Press.

Cook-Sather, A. (2002). Authorizing students' perspectives: Toward trust, dialogue, and change in education. *Educational Researcher, 31*(4), 3–14.

Cuffaro, H. K. (1995). *Experimenting with the world: John Dewey and the early childhood classroom*. New York: Teachers College Press.

Cuffaro, H. K. (2000). *Educational standards in a democratic society: Questioning process and consequences*. Paper presented at the Empowering Teachers Summer Institute, Sarah Lawrence College Child Development Institute, New York.

Damasio, A. (1999). *The feeling of what happens: Body and emotion in the making of consciousness*. New York: Harcourt Brace.

Darling-Hammond, L., Ancess, J., & Falk, B. (1995). *Authentic assessment in action*. New York: Teachers College Press.

Debold, E., Tolman, D., & Brown, L. M. (1996). Embodying knowledge, knowing desire. In N. Goldberger, J. Tarule, B. Clinchy, & M. Belenky (Eds.), *Knowledge, difference, and power* (pp. 85–125). New York: Basic Books.

Delpit, L. (1995). *Other people's children: Cultural conflict in the classroom*. New York: Free Press.

Dewey, J. (1933). *How we think: A restatement of the relation of reflective thinking to the educative process*. Boston: Heath. (Original work published 1910)

Dewey, J. (1963). *Experience and education*. New York: Collier Books and Macmillan. (Original work published 1938)

Dewey, J. (1966). *Democracy and education*. New York: Free Press. (Original work published 1916)

Duckworth, E. (1987). *"The having of wonderful ideas" and other essays on teaching and learning*. New York: Teachers College Press.

Duckworth, E. (2001). *Tell me more: Listening to learners explain*. New York: Teachers College Press.

Eisner, E. (1998). *The enlightened eye: Qualitative inquiry and enhancement of educational practice*. Upper Saddle River, NJ: Merrill/Prentice Hall.

Ekstein, R., & Wallerstein, R. S. (1958). *The teaching and learning of psychotherapy*. New York: Basic Books.

Erikson, E. (1963). *Childhood and society* (2nd ed.). New York: Norton.

Feiman-Nemser, S., Norman, P., & Carroll, D. (2003). *Supporting teachers of teachers: A practice-centered approach to mentor teacher development*. Paper presented at the annual meeting of the American Educational Research Association, Chicago.

Ferguson, A. (2001). *Bad boys: Public schools in the making of black masculinity.*
Ann Arbor: University of Michigan Press.

Fetterly, J. (1978). *The resisting reader: A feminist approach to American fiction.*
Bloomington: University of Indiana Press.

Fine, M. (1996). *Talking across boundaries: Participatory evaluation research in an
urban middle school.* New York: City University of New York Press.

Freeman, D. (1998). *Doing teacher research: From inquiry to understanding.*
Pacific Grove, CA: Heinle & Heinle.

Gardner, H. (1983). *Frames of mind: The theory of multiple intelligences.*
New York: Basic Books.

Gilbert, R., & Gilbert, P. (1998). *Masculinity goes to school.* London and New
York: Routledge.

Gilligan, C. (1991). Teaching Shakespeare's sister: Notes from the underground
of female adolescence. *Women's Studies Quarterly, 29*(1/2).

Gilligan, C. (1993). *In a different voice* (2nd ed.). Cambridge, MA: Harvard
University Press.

Gilligan, C. (1996). Centrality of relationship in human development: A puzzle,
some evidence, and a theory. In G. Noam & K. Fisher (Eds.), *Development
and vulnerability in close relationships* (pp. 237–261). Mahwah, NJ: Erlbaum.

Gilligan, C. (2003). *The birth of pleasure.* New York: Vintage Books.

Gilligan, C. (2004). Knowing and not knowing: Reflections on manhood.
Journal of Psychotherapy and Politics International, 2(2), 99–114.

Gilligan, C., Brown, L. M., & Rogers, A. (1990). Psyche embedded: A place for
body, relationships, and culture in personality theory. In A. I. Rubin & R.
Zucker (Eds.), *Studying persons and lives* (pp. 86–147). New York: Springer.

Gilligan, C., Rogers, A. G., & Noel, N. (1992, February). *Cartography of a lost
time.* Paper presented at the Lilly Endowment Conference on Youth and
Caring, Miami, FL.

Gilligan, C., Rogers, A. G., & Tolman, D. (Eds.). (1991). *Women, girls and
psychotherapy.* New York: Hawthorne Press.

Gilligan, C., Spencer R., Weinberg, M. K., & Bertsch, T. (2003). "On the
listening guide: A voice-centered relational method." In P. M. Camic,
J. E. Rhodes, & L. Yardley (Eds.), *Qualitative research in psychology:
Expanding perspectives in methodology and design* (pp. 157–172).
Washington, DC: American Psychological Association Press.

Gold, J. (1978). *The building of a permanent city: A social studies curriculum for
six- and seven-year-olds.* Unpublished master's thesis, Bank Street College
of Education, New York.

Goldberger, N., Tarule, J., Clinchy, B., & Belenky, M. (Eds.). (1996). *Knowledge, difference and power*. New York: Basic Books.

Goodenow, C. (1992). Strengthening the links between educational psychology and the study of social contexts. *Educational Psychologist, 27*(2), 177–296.

Greene, M. (1973). *Teacher as stranger*. Belmont, CA: Wadsworth.

Haberman, E. (2000). Learning to look closely at children. In N. Nager & E. K. Shapiro (Eds.), *Revisiting a progressive pedagogy* (pp. 203–220). New York: State University of New York Press.

Hansen, J. (1992). Literacy portfolios: Helping students know themselves. *Educational Leadership, 49*, 66–68.

Hawkins, D. (1973). What it means to teach. *Teachers College Record, 73*, 7–16.

Hawkins, D. (1974). I, thou, and it. In D. Hawkins (Ed.), *The informed vision: Essays on learning and human nature* (pp. 48–62). New York: Agathon Press.

Hebert, E. (1992). Portfolios invite reflection from students and staff. *Educational Leadership, 49*, 58–61.

Himley, M., & Carini, P. F. (2000). *From another angle: Children's strengths and school standards*. New York: Teachers College Press.

Howes, C., & Ritchie, S. (2002). *A matter of trust: Connecting teachers and learners in the early childhood classroom*. New York: Teachers College Press.

Jack, D. (1993). *Silencing the self: Women and depression*. New York: Harper Perennial.

Jordan, J. (1991). The meaning of mutuality. In J. Jordan, A. G. Kaplan, J. B. Miller, I. P. Stiver, & J. L. Surrey (Eds.), *Women's growth in connection* (pp. 81–96). New York: Guilford Press.

Jordan, J. (1995). *Relational awareness: Transforming disconnection*. (Work in Progress No. 76). Wellesley, MA: The Stone Center Working Paper Series.

Jordan, J., Kaplan, A. G., Miller, J. B., Stiver, I. P., & Surrey, J. L. (Eds.). (1991). *Women's growth in connection*. New York: Guilford Press.

Kegan, R. (1982). *The evolving self: Problem and process in human development*. Cambridge, MA: Harvard University Press.

Kindlon, D., & Thompson, M. (1999). *Raising Cain: Protecting the emotional life of boys*. New York: Ballantine Books.

Kohlberg, L. (1984). *Essays on moral development: The psychology of moral development* (Vol. 2). San Francisco: Harper & Row.

Kohn, A. (1992). *No contest: The case against competition*. (rev. ed.). Boston: Houghton Mifflin.

Koplow, L. (2002). *Creating schools that heal*. New York: Teachers College Press.

Krechevsky, M. (2001). Form, function, and understanding in learning groups: Propositions from the Reggio classrooms. In Project Zero & Reggio Children, *Making learning visible: Children as individual and group learners* (pp. 246-268). Reggio Emilia, Italy: Reggio Children.

Kriete, R. (2002). *The morning meeting book*. Greenfield, MA: Northeast Foundation for Children.

Kvale, S. (1996). *InterViews*. Thousand Oaks, CA: Sage.

Lawrence-Lightfoot, S. & Davis, J. H. (Eds.). (1997). *The art and science of portraiture*. San Francisco: Jossey-Bass.

Lerner, J. V. (1983). The role of temperament in psychosocial adaptation in early adolescents: A test of a "goodness of fit" model. *Journal of Genetic Psychology, 143*, 149–157.

Lynch, M., & Cicchetti, D. (1997). Children's relationships with adults and peers: An examination of elementary and junior high school students. *Journal of School Psychology, 35*(1), 81–99.

MacLean, M. S. (1983). Voices within: The audience speaks. *English Journal, 72*(7), 62–66.

Malaguzzi, L. (1993). For an education based on relationships. *Young Children, 49*(1), 9–12.

Maslow, A. (1970). *Motivation and personality* (2nd ed.). San Francisco: Harper & Row.

Maxwell, J. A. (1996). *Qualitative research design: An interactive approach*. Thousand Oaks, CA: Sage.

McDermott, R. P. (1977). Social relations as contexts for learning in school. *Harvard Educational Review, 47*(2), 198–213.

Meier, D. (2002). *In schools we trust*. Boston: Beacon Press.

Midgley, C., Feldlaufer, H., & Eccles, J. S. (1989). Student/teacher relations and attitudes before and after the transition to junior high school. *Child Development, 60*, 981–992.

Miller, J. B. (1986). *What do we mean by relationships?* (Work in Progress No. 22). Wellesley, MA: Stone Center Working Paper Series.

Miller, J. B., Jordan, J., Stiver, I. P., Walker, M., Surrey, J., & Eldridge, N. S. (1999). *Therapists' authenticity*. (Work in Progress No. 82). Wellesley, MA: Stone Center Working Paper Series.

Miller, J. B., & Stiver, I. P. (1997). *The healing connection*. Boston: Beacon Press.

Mitchell, R. (1992). *Testing for learning: How new approaches to evaluation can improve American schools*. New York: Free Press.

Murray, L., & Trevarthen, C. (1985). Emotional regulation of interactions between two-month-olds and their mothers. In T. M. Field & N. A. Fox (Eds.), *Social perception in infants* (pp. 177–197). Norwood, NJ: Ablex.

Nager, N., & Shapiro, E. K. (Eds.). (2000). *Revisiting a progressive pedagogy.* New York: State University of New York Press.

Noddings, N. (2003). *Caring: A feminine approach to ethics and moral education* (2nd ed.). Berkeley: University of California Press.

Orenstein, P. (1994). *School girls: Young women, self-esteem, and the confidence gap.* New York: Doubleday.

Paley, V. (1986a). *Molly is three.* Cambridge, MA: Harvard University Press.

Paley, V. (1986b). On listening to what children say. *Harvard Educational Review, 56*(2), 122–131.

Paley, V. (1990). *The boy who would be a helicopter.* Cambridge, MA: Harvard University Press.

Paley, V. (1991). *Wally's stories.* Cambridge, MA: Harvard University Press.

Paley, V. (2004). *A child's work: The importance of fantasy play.* Chicago: University of Chicago Press.

Paris, S. G., & Ayres, L. A. (1994). *Becoming reflective students and teachers with portfolios and authentic assessment.* Washington, DC: American Psychological Association.

Paris, S. G., & Newman, R. S. (1990). Developmental aspects of self-regulated learning. *Educational Psychologist, 25*(1), 87–102.

Patrick, H. (1997). Social self-regulation: Exploring the relations between children's social relationships, academic self-regulation, and school performance. *Educational Psychologist, 32*(4), 209–220.

Perrone, V. (Ed.). (1991). *Expanding student assessment.* Alexandria, VA: Association for Supervision and Curriculum Development.

Perrone, V. (1998). *Teacher with a heart: Reflections on Leonard Covello and community.* New York: Teachers College Press.

Perrotti, J., & Westheimer, K. (2001). *When the drama club is not enough: Lessons from the Safe Schools Program for Gay and Lesbian Students.* New York: Beacon Press.

Piaget, J. (1963). *The origins of intelligence in children.* New York: Norton. (Original work published 1952)

Piaget, J. (1969). *The child's conception of the world.* Totowa, NJ: Littlefield, Adams & Co. (Original work published 1929)

Piaget, J. (1970). *Genetic epistemology.* New York: Columbia University Press.

Pianta, R. (1999). *Enhancing relationships between children and teachers*. Washington, DC: American Psychological Association Press.

Pipher, M. (1994). *Reviving Ophelia: Saving the selves of adolescent girls*. New York: Ballantine Books.

Pollack, W. (1998). *Real boys: Rescuing our sons from the myths of boyhood*. New York: Henry Holt.

Pollack, W. (2000). *Real boys' voices*. New York: Random House.

Project Zero, Harvard Graduate School of Education. (2001). *The evidence process: A collaborative approach to understanding and improving teaching and learning*. Cambridge, MA: Author.

Raider-Roth, M. (1995a). *Daria: Interview 1*. Unpublished manuscript, Harvard Graduate School of Education, Cambridge, MA.

Raider-Roth, M. (1995b). *Emily: Summary of a voice centered relational analysis*. Unpublished manuscript, Harvard Graduate School of Education, Cambridge, MA.

Raider-Roth, M. (1995c). *Jon: Summary of a voice centered relational analysis*. Unpublished manuscript, Harvard Graduate School of Education, Cambridge, MA.

Raider-Roth, M. (2003). *Knowing their journey: Understanding the complexities of teaching boys, a documentary account*. Paper presented at the annual meeting of the American Educational Research Association, Chicago.

Raider-Roth, M. (2004). Taking the time to think: A portrait of reflection. *Teaching & Learning: The Journal of Natural Inquiry and Reflective Practice, 18*(3), 79–97.

Raider-Roth, M. (2005). Trusting what you know: Negotiating the relational complexities of classroom life. *Teachers College Record, 107*(4).

Raider-Roth, M., Ball, K., Carini, P. F., Cruz-Acosta, L., Gutman, S., Merrett, S., Onishi, T., & Waithe, W. (2003). *Using descriptive process as a lens to race and school culture: A work in progress*. (2003). Paper presented at annual meeting of the North Dakota Study Group on Evaluation, Cambridge, MA.

Real, T. (1998). *I don't want to talk about it: Overcoming the secret legacy of male depression*. New York: Scribner.

Rodgers, C. R. (2002a). Defining reflection: Another look at John Dewey and reflective thinking. *Teachers College Record. 104*(4), 842–866.

Rodgers, C. R. (2002b). Seeing student learning: Teacher change and the role of reflection. *Harvard Educational Review, 72*(2), 230–253.

Rodgers, C. R., & Raider-Roth, M. (2004). *Presence in teaching*. Paper presented at the annual meeting of the American Educational Research Association, San Diego, CA.

Roeser, R. W., Eccles, J. S., & Sameroff, A. J. (2000). School as a context of early adolescents' academic and social-emotional development: A summary of research findings. *Elementary School Journal, 100*(5), 443–471.

Rogers, A. (1993). Voice, play, and a practice of ordinary courage in girls' and women's lives. *Harvard Educational Review, 63,* 265–295.

Rogers, A., Brown, L. M., & Tappan, M. (1993). *Interpreting loss in ego development in girls: Regression or resistance?* Paper presented at the annual meeting of the American Psychological Association, San Francisco.

Rogoff, B. (1990). *Apprenticeship in thinking.* New York: Oxford University Press.

Ross, J. A., Hogabaum-Gray, A., & Rolheiser, C. (2002). Student self-evaluation in grade 5–6 mathematics effects on problem-solving achievement. *Educational Assessment, 8*(1), 43–59.

Schultz, K. (2003). *Listening: A framework for teaching across differences.* New York: Teachers College Press.

Schunk, D. H. (1990). Goal setting and self-efficacy during self-regulated learning. *Educational Psychologist, 25*(1), 71–86.

Schunk, D. H. (1996). *Self-evaluation and self-regulated learning* (ERIC Document 403 233). New York: City University of New York.

Schunk, D. H., & Zimmerman, B. J. (1997). Social origins of self-regulatory competence. *Educational Psychologist, 32*(4), 195–208.

Seidel, S. (1998). Learning from looking. In N. Lyons (Ed.), *With portfolio in hand* (pp. 69–89). New York: Teachers College Press.

Seidel, S., Walters, J., Kirby, E., Olff, N., Powell, K., Scripp, L., & Veenema, S. (1997). *Portfolio practices: Thinking through the assessment of children's work.* Washington, DC: National Education Association.

Seidman, I. (1998). *Interviewing as qualitative research.* New York: Teachers College Press.

Shifter, D., Bastable, V., & Russell, S. J. (1999). *Developing mathematical ideas: Building a systems of tens.* Parsippany, NJ: EDC/Dale Seymour.

Spencer, R. (2000). *A comparison of relational psychologies.* (Project Report No. 5). Wellesley, MA: Stone Center Working Paper Series.

Stern, D. (1985). *The interpersonal world of the infant.* New York: Basic Books.

Stiggins, R. J. (2002). Assessment crisis: The absence of assessment FOR learning. *Phi Delta Kappan, 83*(10), 758–765.

Strieb, L. (1985). *A (Philadelphia) teacher's journal.* Grand Forks: North Dakota Study Group on Evaluation.

Surrey, J. L. (1991). The "self-in-relation": A theory of women's development. In J. Jordan, A. Kaplan, J. B. Miller, I. Stiver, & J. Surrey (Eds.), *Women's growth in connection: Writings from the Stone Center* (pp. 51-66). New York: Guilford Press.

Tai, B. (1999). *Manifest power: Toward a relational psychology of teaching.* Unpublished dissertation, Harvard Graduate School of Education, Cambridge, MA.

Tappan, M. (2001). Interpretive psychology: Stories, circles, and understanding lived experience. In D. Tolman & M. Brydon-Miller (Eds.), *From subjects to subjectivities: A handbook of interpretive and participatory methods* (pp. 45–56). New York: New York University Press.

Taylor, J. M., Gilligan, C., & Sullivan, A. M. (1995). *Between voice and silence: Women and girls, race and relationship.* Cambridge, MA: Harvard University Press.

Thomas, A., & Chess, S. (1977). *Temperament and development.* New York: Brunner/Mazel.

Tierney, R. J., Carter, M. A., & Desai, L. E. (1991). *Portfolio assessment in the reading-writing classroom.* Norwood, MA: Christopher-Gordon.

Tolman, D. (2002). *Dilemmas of desire: Teenage girls talk about sexuality.* Cambridge, MA: Harvard University Press.

Towler, L., & Broadfoot, P. (1992). Self-assessment in the primary school. *Educational Review, 44*(2), 137–151.

Trevarthen, C. (1979). Communication and cooperation in early infancy: A description of primary intersubjectivity. In M. Bullowa (Ed.), *Before speech: The beginnings of interpersonal communication* (pp. 321–347). Cambridge, England: Cambridge University Press.

Tronick, E. Z. (1989). Emotions and emotional communication in infants. *American Psychologist, 44*(2), 112–119.

Tronick, E. Z., & Weinberg, M. K. (1997). Depressed mothers and infants: Failure to form dyadic states of consciousness. In L. Murray & P. Cooper (Eds.), *Postpartum depression and child development* (pp. 54–81). New York: Guilford Press.

van Kraayenoord, C. E., & Paris, S. G. (1993, December). *Self-assessment: Children's perspectives on their literacy activities in the classroom.* Paper presented at the 43rd annual meeting of the National Reading Conference, Charleston, SC.

van Kraayenoord, C. E., & Paris, S. G. (1997). Australian students' self-appraisal of their work samples and academic progress. *Elementary School Journal, 97*(5), 523–537.

Veenema, S., Hetland, L., & Chalfen, K. (Eds.). (1997). *The Project Zero classroom: New approaches to thinking and understanding.* Cambridge, MA: Project Zero, Harvard Graduate School of Education.

Vygotsky, L. S. (1978). *Mind in society.* Cambridge, MA: Harvard University Press.

Walker, B. J. (2003). The cultivation of student self-efficacy in reading and writing. *Reading and Writing Quarterly, 19,* 1731–1787.

Walters, J., Seidel, S., & Gardner, H. (1994). Children as reflective practitioners: Bringing metacognition to the classroom. In J. N. Mangieri & C. C. Block (Eds.), *Creating powerful thinking in teachers and students: Diverse perspectives* (pp. 289–303). Fort Worth, TX: Harcourt Brace College.

Ward, J. (2001). *The skin we're in: Teaching our children to be socially smart, emotionally strong, spiritually connected.* New York: Free Press.

Watson, M., & Ecken, L. (2003). *Learning to trust: Transforming difficult elementary classrooms through developmental discipline.* San Francisco: Jossey-Bass.

Way, N. (1998). *Everyday courage.* New York: New York University Press.

Way, N., & Chu, J. (2004). *Adolescent boys: Exploring diverse cultures in boyhood.* New York: New York University Press.

Weinbaum, A., Allen, D., Blythe, T., Simon, K., Seidel, S., & Rubin, C. (2004). *Teaching as inquiry: Asking hard questions to improve practice and student achievement.* New York: Teachers College Press.

Wertsch, J. V. (1985). Adult-child interaction as a source of self-regulation in children. In S. R. Yussen (Ed.), *The growth of reflection in children* (pp. 69–97). Orlando, FL: Academic Press.

Winnicott, D. W. (1965). The theory of parent-infant relationship. In D. W. Winnicott (Ed.), *The maturational processes and the facilitating environment: Studies in the theory of emotional development* (pp. 37–55). New York: International Universities Press.

Wiske, M. S. (Ed.). (1998). *Teaching for understanding: Linking research with practice.* San Francisco: Jossey-Bass.

Zessoules, R., & Gardner, H. (1991). Authentic assessment: Beyond the buzzword. In V. Perrone (Ed.), *Expanding student assessment* (pp. 47–71). Alexandria, VA: Association for Supervision and Curriculum Development.

Index

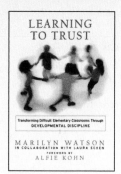

Learning to Trust
Transforming Difficult Elementary Classrooms Through Developmental Discipline

Marylyn Watson and Laura Ecken

ISBN: 0-7879-6650-9   Cloth
www.josseybass.com

"In this book, Marilyn Watson has taken years of experience, wedded it to a deep understanding of child development, and applied a powerful ability to listen and interpret the experience of one remarkable and courageous teacher, Laura Ecken. Together, Marilyn and Laura show us all a more enlightened way to work with challenging children in schools. The unique application of attachment theory to classroom management and discipline offers all educators a new vision for fostering healthy classrooms and children of character."
— Marvin W. Berkowitz, Sanford N. McDonnell Professor of Character Education, College of Education, University of Missouri-St. Louis

This book applies attachment theory to the school setting, showing how this perspective can help teachers build collaborative, trusting relationships even with their most challenging students. Marilyn Sheehan Watson explains and describes the ups and downs of Laura Ecken's classroom through the lens of attachment theory, while Laura describes in vivid detail the ongoing life of her classroom, revealing throughout her challenges, thoughts, fears, failures, and successes. Together they explore strategies for helping children develop the emotional skills needed to live harmonious and productive lives, the social and communication skills to be a friend and work collaboratively with classmates, the self confidence and curiosity to invest wholeheartedly in learning, and the empathy and personal and moral understanding to be caring and responsible young people.

Learning to Trust will help teachers meet the challenge to care, balance their need for authority with their students' need for autonomy, and support their students' intellectual growth without abandoning their obligation to educate for responsible citizenship and an ethical life.

Marilyn Sheehan Watson has worked for more than two decades with teachers, teacher educators, and education researchers to effectively promote children's social, moral, and intellectual development. As program director of the Developmental Studies Center's award-winning school change effort, the Child Development Project, and as director of the center's national Teacher Education Project, she has been instrumental in defining education that has children's basic developmental needs at its heart.

Laura Ecken has shared sixteen thoughtful years with the elementary school children of Louisville, Kentucky. She is one of the teachers we never forget.

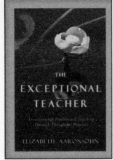

The Exceptional Teacher
Transforming Traditional Teaching
Through Thoughtful Practice

Elizabeth Aaronsohn

ISBN: 0-7879-6576-6 Cloth
www.josseybass.com

The Exceptional Teacher offers new approaches to preparing teachers so they will be able to break free from outmoded habits and methods, and become teachers who encourage their students to learn independently, creatively, and collaboratively.

In *The Exceptional Teacher,* veteran K–12 teacher Elizabeth Aaronsohn examines three important questions: What do our teachers really want our children to get out of school? How do their own schooling experiences inhibit them from achieving these goals? How can a teacher education program give beginning teachers a framework for thinking differently about the whole process of teaching?

The Exceptional Teacher offers the guidance that teacher educators need to help their students become teachers who are knowledgeable and skillful practitioners, while also developing the ability to be reflective, imaginative, courageous, and flexible in the classroom—a model for the students they are instructing. In this inspiring book, Aaronsohn shows that becoming an exceptional teacher can be a difficult but rewarding journey. She explains that success begins in understanding one's self and societal and cultural experiences. Based on qualitative research from student writings and workshops, the author offers practical advice to help beginning teachers move beyond their own internalized assumptions, and become educators who will transform their classrooms.

Aaronsohn encourages teachers to develop the practice of honest reflection on their attitudes, thinking, and practices, and especially to develop the capacity to assume the perspective of another person. These practices can be nurtured through the process of in-depth writing, which helps to make meaning of experiences and brings teachers to a new level of consciousness about themselves, the world, and the mission of teaching.

Elizabeth Aaronsohn is an associate professor of teacher education at Central Connecticut State University in New Britain, Connecticut. She has taught eight years each at three levels: high school English; college English, speech, and women's studies; and early elementary school. She is the author of *Going Against the Grain: Supporting the Student-Centered Teacher.*

Finders and Keepers
Helping New Teachers Survive and Thrive in Our Schools
Susan Moore Johnson and The Project on the Next Generation of Teachers

ISBN: 0-7879-6925-7 Cloth
www.josseybass.com

U.S. public schools face the unprecedented challenge of recruiting, supporting, and retaining more than 2.2 million new teachers over the next decade. These new teachers may well staff the nation's schools until mid-century. Whether they will be qualified, committed, and effective will depend on the decisions and actions taken by policymakers, education officials, school leaders, and individual teachers across the country. *Finders and Keepers* not only explores the difficulties new teachers face and offers rich cases and informed insight into their experiences, but also provides practical recommendations about how to best attract and retain a strong teaching force.

This important and much-needed book is based on a longitudinal study of fifty new teachers during their first years in the classroom. It highlights the cases of ten, whose stories vividly illustrate the joys and disappointments of new teachers in today's schools. The book documents why they entered teaching, what they encountered in their schools, and how they decided whether to stay or move on to other schools or other lines of work. By tracking these teachers' eventual career decisions, *Finders and Keepers* reveals what really matters to new teachers as they set out to educate their students. The book uncovers the importance of the school site and the crucial role that principals and experienced teachers play in the effective hiring and induction of the next generation of teachers.

Staffing the nation's schools presents both challenges and opportunities. For teacher educators, district administrators, educational policymakers, teachers, principals, and staff development professionals, *Finders and Keepers* provides valuable insights about how to better serve new teachers and the students they teach.

Susan Moore Johnson, a former high school teacher and administrator, is the Pforzheimer Professor of Teaching and Learning at the Harvard Graduate School of Education, where from 1993 to 1999 she served as academic dean. Johnson is a member of the National Academy of Education and director of The Project on the Next Generation of Teachers. She is the author of numerous articles and several books, including *Leading to Change* (Jossey-Bass).

Through Ebony Eyes
What Teachers Need to Know But Are Afraid
to Ask About African American Students
Gail L. Thompson

ISBN: 0-7879-7061-1 Cloth
www.josseybass.com

"For those teachers, administrators, and researchers who deal with culturally sensitive issues, *Through Ebony Eyes* is a powerful tool. Gail Thompson writes with passion and authority on teachers' beliefs and attitudes regarding African American students, and how these affect their instructional practices and achievement. Her research and observations are insightful, and her recommendations essential."

—James P. Comer, M.D., Maurice Falk Professor of Child Psychiatry,
Yale Child Study Center, associate dean, School of Medicine

In this book, Gail L. Thompson takes on the volatile topic of the role of race in education and explores the black-white achievement gap and the cultural divide that exists between some teachers and African American students. Solidly based on research conducted with 175 educators, Thompson provides information and strategies that will help teachers increase their effectiveness with African American students. Written in conversational language, *Through Ebony Eyes* offers a wealth of examples and personal stories that clearly demonstrate the cultural differences that exist in the schools and offers a three-part, long-term professional development plan that will help teachers become more effective.

Gail L. Thompson is associate professor of education at Claremont Graduate University. Her research has focused on the schooling experiences of students of color. She is the author of *African American Teens Discuss Their Schooling Experiences* and *What African American Parents Want Educators to Know*, as well as numerous journal articles.